is for

Atticus

A is for

Atticus

Baby Names from Great Books

Lorilee Craker

CENTER
STREET

NEW YORK   BOSTON   NASHVILLE

Center Street
Hachette Book Group USA
237 Park Avenue
New York, NY 10017

Visit our Web site at www.centerstreet.com.

Center Street is a division of Hachette Book Group USA, Inc.
The Center Street name and logo are trademarks of Hachette Book Group USA, Inc.

Printed in the United States of America

First Edition: August 2008

10 9 8 7 6 5 4 3 2 1

Library of Congress Cataloging-in-Publication Data

Craker, Lorilee.
    A is for Atticus : baby names from great books / Lorilee Craker. — 1st ed.
       p. cm.
    Summary: "A fresh collection of dynamic, modern, and meaningful literary names selected from great books."—Provided by the publisher
    ISBN-13: 978-1-59995-020-4
    ISBN-10: 1-59995-020-0
    1. Names, Personal—Dictionaries. 2. Characters and characteristics in literature—Dictionaries. 3. Names in literature—Dictionaries. I. Title.

CS2377.C725 2008
929.4'4—dc22

                          2007037912

To Jonah Abram Reimer, Ezra Finney Brandt,

and Phoebe Min-Ju Jayne:

By any other names you would still be

God's best gifts to Daddy and me.

Acknowledgments

To the following people, my abiding thanks and a latte for their personal encouragement and for helping me in some way write this book I so loved:

Linda Reimer, Rachel Arnold, Sheri Rodriguez, Ann Byle, Shelly Beach, Tracy Groot, Angela Blyker, Alison Hodgson, Cynthia Beach, Katrina De Man, Sharon Carrns, Mary Jo Haab, Nancy Rubin, Chip MacGregor, Chris Park, Lori Quinn, and Linda Van Steinvoorn. Everyone at Hachette Book Group and Center Street Books.

Special thanks to Sarah Sper, who championed this book from day one and has been a dream editor every step of the way. Also, I am grateful to Debra Rienstra, professor of English at Calvin College, for her scholarly input and for placing *The Faerie Queene* on my radar, and to the staff at Pooh's Corner, especially Sally Bulthuis, Camille DeBoer, and Margaret Bulgarella, for their boundless enthusiasm for children's books.

And extra-special thanks to Doyle, Jonah, Ezra, and Phoebe Craker for giving me their keen opinions on the names in this book, and mostly for loving me so well through the writing of it.

Contents

Contents

Boys 105

Index 203

About the Author 217

Introduction

I f "so many books, so little time" is your mantra, you'll find a wealth of baby-name ideas from the stories and characters you love.

You know what to expect from baby-name books: an endless, dull list of names with their dictionary definitions. Millions of prospective parents thumb through these dry tomes every year in search of the perfect name for their perfect baby.

As the author of eight parenting books, including one baby-name book, one question I get all the time is this: "How can our baby's name really mean something to us beyond just the fact that it sounds nice?" Today's baby namers want their offspring's ID to reflect some character quality, cultural heritage, spiritual reference, or some slice of family history that is deeply meaningful to them. The Bible is a fantastic source of such names, as I discovered while naming my own brood, but another untapped gold mine is your bookshelf, filled with dog-eared, spine-cracked, loved-on books that mean so much to you.

Enter *A is for Atticus*, which of course is inspired by the unflinchingly just Atticus Finch from the book many folks consider their all-time favorite: *To Kill a Mockingbird*.

Quality Over Quantity

Interesting fact: Research shows the vast majority of parents-to-be pluck their name choice from the same list of five hundred names. That means people don't actually need the encyclopedia-size book with five thousand choices. It's like the huge menu you feel you have to pore over, when meanwhile what you really need is fewer choices—and more information about each choice!

A is for Atticus gives bookish parents quality over quantity. It is an earthy guide to heavenly names, profiling the most gorgeous, viable, and meaningful names from great books.

Recently, I came across a literature junkie who dubbed his son Yeats in honor of the poet. Friends conferred the Shakespearean name Ariel on their daughter, and other pals got names for their Little Women, Josephine and Louisa, from a favorite childhood classic. I also know more than one young woman who never forgot the adventures of the irrepressible red-haired orphan from Prince Edward Island, Anne of Green Gables: they gave their daughters the middle or first name Anne, "with an *e*" of course!

And my name, Lorilee, is actually rooted in my mom's

girlhood penchant for reading the Bobbsey Twins books by Laura Lee Hope.

Yes, you want a name for your baby that is fresh, beautiful, and suited stylistically to your tastes. But you also want something more. Given the feedback from my first baby-name book, *A Is for Adam*, I know that when parents dub their babies with Bible names, they hope that Noah's faith, Lydia's industriousness, Tabitha's kindness, or Caleb's boldness will rub off on their namesakes—or at least inspire them to live up to the best qualities their names evoke. Truly, the characters we love from the books we cherish inspire the same kind of wishes for their namesakes.

Celebrity Trend

Want proof that lit names are white hot? Check out the list below of star babies with librarian-approved IDs. Why star babies? Celebs, for better or worse, have become our culture's pioneers when it comes to what we name our babies. (Example: Eight years ago, Heather Locklear and Richie Sambora dusted off Ava, a glamorous yet musty name from the props trunks on the studio lots of the 1940s. Today, Ava is number 10 on the top 100 names in the USA, and thank-you notes go to Heather and Richie. People who have never seen Locklear on the tube or Sambora in one Bon Jovi concert or video nonetheless grew fond of Ava through hearing it over and over again.) This is how names filter through Tinseltown and eventually end up in Tacoma, Toronto, and Topeka. Check out how the trendsetters have latched on to literary names in their quest for the hippest and the hottest:

- Eliot/Elliott (for a girl)   Sting and Trudie Styler,
  George Stephanopoulos and
  Ali Wentworth
- Gulliver   Gary Oldman
- Truman   Tom Hanks and Rita Wilson
- Atticus   Isabella Hofmann and Daniel
  Baldwin
- Scout   Demi Moore and Bruce Willis
- Esme   Michael J. Fox and Tracy Pollan
- Zelda   Robin Williams
- Harper   George Stephanopoulos and
  Ali Wentworth

In-Depth Name Profiles

A is for Atticus answers the questions that plague pregnant women during sleepless nights of kicks and muscle spasms, and also occur to their husbands in broad daylight:

- How popular is this name, and how will this affect my child? (Emma is the number one name in the country. Will my little Emma be one of six in her playgroup?)
- What are other people going to think about my baby (and me) based on his name?
- Will my child be teased for having a truly unique literary name, like Gulliver or Moby?

Instead of just listing names (*yawn*), each name selected for *A is for Atticus* is profiled for its uniqueness, image, and whether or not it is up-and-coming or more stale than last week's doughnuts. Some listings include other pertinent, real-world info, such as ambigender options, cultural spins, and nicknames

Each name's profile packs these kinds of details—what you really want to know—in a fun, savvy, info-packed listing.

Something for Everyone

- Classic name lovers: **Charles** (Dickens), **Laura** (Ingalls Wilder), **William** (Shakespeare), **Alice** (Walker, *in Wonderland*), **Samuel** (Beckett, Longhorne Clemens, Taylor Coleridge), **Anna** (Karenina), **Arthur** (King Arthur)
- Top 20 types: **Emily** (Dickinson), **Emma** (Jane Austen), **Jordan** (*The Great Gatsby*), **Madeline** (from the classic French children's books), **Nicholas** (Nickleby), **Austen** (Jane), and **Dylan** (Thomas)
- "Goldilocks" baby namers (not too hot, not too cold): **Lucy** (*Mansfield Park*), **Chloe** (Longus), and **Lily** (*To the Lighthouse*, Woolf), **Tess** (*of the d'Urbervilles*), **Owen**, **Nathaniel** (Hawthorne), **Sebastian** (*The Tempest*, *Twelfth Night*)

And for those who are willing to scale mountain peaks and dredge the deepest rivers (or just go out on a limb) for a peerless name for their peerless progeny:

- **Gulliver** (of *Travels* fame), **Atticus** (*To Kill a Mockingbird*), **Truman** (Capote), **Yeats**, **Esmé** (from the short story by J. D. Salinger, "For Esmé—with Love and Squalor"), **Eliot** (for a girl, to honor T. S. Eliot), **Flannery** (O'Connor), and **Harper** (Lee, *To Kill a Mockingbird*)

This little tome is for many ethnic backgrounds. **Langston** (Hughes), **Maya** (Angelou), **Booker** (T. Washington), and **Zora** (Neale Hurston) are just a few of the names African American parents use to weave their heritage into their baby's name. There are also plenty of Irish, Scottish, Scandinavian, German, Jewish, and Latino names to choose from. Lit names that are also ethnic tributes allow you to kill two birds with one stone. Now that's savvy baby naming!

Fellow book addict, I hope you will enjoy all the fun little literary tidbits in these pages even half as much as I grooved on collecting them. I fell in love all over again with some of my childhood favorites, and I discovered new treasures as well. During the writing of this book, I read such diverse classics as *A Tree Grows in Brooklyn* by Betty Smith, *Pride and Prejudice* by Jane Austen, *The Heart Is a Lonely Hunter* by Carson McCullers, and *Daddy-Long-Legs* by Jean Webster. From these stellar reads I gleaned names such as Lizzie, Georgianna, Portia, and Jerusha.

I saw *The Tempest* onstage and was thrilled to see "my" characters (i.e.: lit namesakes from this book), such as Miranda, Iris, and Antonio, come alive. And speaking of Shakespeare, the man was a supremely gifted name-giver. Some of my best-loved names in this collection are from his imagination, including Lennox, Tarquin, Phoebe, and Marina.

Lest you think this is a highbrow assortment of names gathered by someone who lies around the house reading Homer and Spencer, it's not. Thankfully, I do have some scholarly pals who kicked in some fabulous name ideas from their ponderous minds, and I also know my way around a certain nifty children's bookstore, where many abiding pieces of the repertoire were brought to my attention. But most of all, I love books, and one of the greatest gifts of my life has been plunging into the lives and adventures of fantastic characters. I consider Anne of Green Gables to be a mentor, Jane Austen to be a writing hero, and the Bard a fellow name freak like myself.

The writing process, then, which combined my bookworm's soul with my addiction to all things name related, was pure joy. (During the months I wrote, I ran into a teenage Atticus, a toddler Silas, and a baby Zelda, and I had to restrain myself from breaking into song.) If any of you e-mail me and tell me you have named your son Lucan (a great discovery, I thought) or Odessa (an equally fascinating "find"), I will probably do a jig in my kitchen, alarming my family and the pets. But e-mail me anyway, because they are used to being alarmed at my behavior.

So pick a winner, then, dear reader, and have a wonderful time doing so. May God bless you as you choose a singular designation for your singular, precious baby.

—*Lorilee Craker*

———

Girls

———

A

Abigail: With a beautiful, antique sound, deep biblical roots, and a meaning that rocks—"Father's joy"—Abigail has the whole package, and it shows in the name's mega-popularity. Currently leasing a spot on the top 10, Abigail is phenomenally well liked, but its saving grace is a classic stature that will never sound dated, even though it's currently overdone. Abigail, which used to be slang for a female servant, is a waiting woman character in Beaumont and Fletcher's 1616 comedy *The Scornful Lady*.

Nickname: Abby

Abra: Abra, the feminine version of Abram, has a pure, ethereal sound. It's imaginative, singular, and is even infused with literary essence thanks to John Steinbeck's capricious character in *East of Eden*. When all of Abra's positives are considered, it seems like a glorious designation for a baby girl. But, yes, I know: "a bra." Some short wise guys out there will have a ball with that—for ten minutes. If you decide your little Abra can handle this—after all, teasing is short-lived—people will likely think of your daughter as being creative and artistic before they even meet her. Such is the innovative power Abra carries.

Addison: This "new" spin on the fading Madison is one of the hottest names out there, thanks to the character on the hit television series *Grey's Anatomy* and *Private Practice*. Though this name will burn brightly for a few years before its popularity levels off, it has more than just trite television ties: Joseph Addison wrote his most famous play, titled *Cato: A Tragedy* in 1712.

Nickname: Addie

If you like super-trendy Addison, consider Adelaide, Adeline, or Emerson for a less faddish option.

Adela: Looking for something really quaint? Go for this old-fashioned but perkier variation on the dormant Adele. The main character of E. M. Forster's *A Passage to India*, a British schoolmistress who becomes embroiled in a crime case while traveling in India is named Adela, perhaps after the medieval queen Adela of Normandy.

Nickname: Addie

Adelaide: A very cool way to circumvent the meteor Addison and still arrive at the nickname Addie is to go with this lyrical moniker. Adelaide is a city in Australia, which was named after "Good Queen Adelaide," the wife of King

William IV of England. It's a nineteenth-century antique restoration, and a name with character and charm to spare. In the Wombles books by Elisabeth Beresford, Miss Adelaide was the green (much ahead of her time) schoolmistress of the furry creatures that live in the burrow of Wimbledon Common.

Nickname: Addie

Agatha: Though I loved my Oma Agatha very much, I always thought she had the clunkiest name of all time—that is until, one day, I saw an exquisite little bookshop: Aunt Agatha's New & Used Mysteries, Detection & True Crime Books. My perception began to change, and today I consider Agatha one of the eccentric grand dames (along with Harriet, Matilda, and Louise). This is just right for parents who want to buck the fashionable name trends. Can't you just see a darling little screwball/sassy pants with the name Agatha? You can even shorten it to the saucier Aggie. Someday you could take a pint-size Aggie to Aunt Agatha's bookshop and tell her all about Dame Agatha Christie, Lady Mallowan, the best-selling book author of all time. Born Agatha Mary Clarissa in 1890, Christie was an English crime fiction writer. The "Queen of Crime" immortalized detectives Hercule Poirot and Miss Marple

---

Mod and Marvelous Middles

Blue ❈ Doone ❈ Echo ❈ Iris ❈ Juno ❈ Luna ❈ Marlowe
❈ Maud ❈ May ❈ Nell ❈ Scout ❈ Tess ❈ Willa

---

and gave countless mystery lovers ample reasons to burn the midnight oil until they discovered at last *whodunnit*.

Nickname: Aggie

Agnes: If you thought Harriet, Matilda, and Stella were wacky, prepare yourself for a possible Agnes revival. This dowdy old clunker, once a top 40 hit at the turn of the century, is so moldering and unwieldy it actually has a shot at refurbishment. (What's next? Edna? Ethel?) Actress Elisabeth Shue and her husband, Davis Guggenheim, chose Agnes Charles for their baby girl (which just goes to show you never know which way the wind blows when it comes to celebrity baby names). And Aggie's cute, especially for a Texas A&M fan. Charles Dickens's *David Copperfield* has a character named Agnes.

Nickname: Aggie

Aine: Pronounced "Anya," this is a pretty Irish word name meaning "splendor, radiance, and brilliance." Aine is connected with abundance and success. In Irish legend, Aine was the queen of the Munster fairies and was one of the wives of Finn Mac Cool. Aine appears in folktales as "the best-hearted woman who ever lived—lucky in love and in money." You can't do much better than that.

Alexandra: Stately Alexandra never goes out of style. It's got beauty, depth, and steel in its spine, a winning blend that has caused parents to choose it with pride for the past few decades. Lately, the name has slipped in popularity, which means it isn't as prevalent anymore as it was in the 1990s. Alexandra Bergson was the strong and inspir-

ing Swedish immigrant farmer in Willa
Cather's *O Pioneers!*

Nicknames: Alex, Lexi

Alice: People may be slightly wonder-filled
if you pick Alice—isn't it an old-school,
musty name? Yes, it is, and that's the
appeal! Stuffy oldies Violet and Frances
have made huge strides forward, and Alice
is following suit, rising slowly but steadily.
Ever since Lewis Carroll's enchanting heroine ducked down the rabbit hole in his
1865 classic *Alice's Adventures in Wonderland*, Alice has brought to mind adventure
and whimsy. You can hardly choose a more loved and en-
joyed character in literature to name your child after, and
Alice's capers will always be special to your daughter—and
to you.

> If you like Alexandra, Arabella, Anabel, and Antonia are more novel choices.

Amelia: So many parents have chosen this turn-of-the-
century beauty as an alternative to Emily that it has almost
become overused itself. Almost. But, like Emily, Amelia is
such a stalwart classic no one can accuse it of being trendy.
And though Amelia continues to ascend, possibly hitting
the top 50 anytime, it will always have the feel of an heirloom, no matter how popular it gets. Amelia was a character in Thackery's *Vanity Fair*.

Nickname: Melia, Ammie

Amoret: The lushly romantic Amoret takes Amory one
step further. Unlike Amory, it's a female name that dates

back at least to 1596, when Edmund Spenser published his six-book epic poem *The Faerie Queene*. Amoret represents the virtue of married love, and her marriage to Scudamour (though interrupted by the little matter of a wedding-night kidnapping) stands as an example of loyalty and stick-to-it-iveness in matrimony. She is eventually rescued by **Britomart,** a female knight in shining armor who represents chastity. Girl power!

Amory: Avery, Amanda, and Emily all sound kind of done at this point, so how about similar-sounding Amory? Like Avery, Amory is a traditionally male name with all the cross-over potential in the world, but because it's never been used much for boys, the door is wide open to grab it for the girls. F. Scott Fitzgerald's main character in *This Side of Paradise*, Amory Blaine, is said to have been based on himself.

Anna: Anna is a *Little House on the Prairie* name, which brings to mind a pioneer who left her homeland to toil by day under the hot sun and sleep at night under a sod roof. Though she is climbing the popularity charts, this stylish classic has the backbone to withstand the trendy tempests of Ashley and Aubrey: there's nothing froufrou about Anna. The name means "full of grace" and has been bestowed upon countless literary heroines, chiefly Tolstoy's formidable heroine Anna Karenina. Refined, intelligent, and imbued with an unmistakable European charm, Anna is the ideal choice for those who want to honor relatives from the old country or for those who simply want a strong name for their daughter.

Anne: Take another peek at this sleek, ageless stalwart. Say it out loud, and it really has the softest, prettiest sound. But you must use an *e* at the end, especially if you loved the irrepressible, carrot-topped orphan Anne of Green Gables. Many young mothers have bestowed this clean-cut classic as a middle name to honor Anne with an *e*, but it also makes an elegant first name. Anne is a character in *Persuasion*, a novel by Jane Austen, as well as reams of other fiction; the moniker also belonged to the youngest Brontë sister, author of two novels.

Antonia: If Ashley and Alyssa are pink lemonade names, Antonia suggests the rich, frothy café hues of an espresso. It's swish without being swag, a richly textured classic that has never been overused. Many critics consider *My Ántonia* to be Willa Cather's finest achievement. Her creation of the bohemian immigrant Ántonia Shimerda is a tribute to the proud, hardworking women pioneers who helped build the West. There are a few nickname options here, but Nia is the only acceptable deconstruction. Antonia is glorious as it is.
Nicknames: Nia

Anya: You take Anna out to the Russian Tea Room and this exotic-around-the-edges beauty emerges. This works, too, if you want to pay tribute to a Polish, German, Dutch, or Eastern European background. Anya is very pretty, quite simple, and yet still has the faint swish of twirling peasant skirts with vibrant embroidery. It has one foot in the old world and one foot in the new. Anya was in Chekhov's *The Cherry Orchard*.

Arabella: Isabella is white hot (and waaaaay overused), so let's consider Arabella, which is every bit as sumptuous and gorgeous but a genuine nineteenth-century rarity. The bonus here is that you still get ultracute Bella (or Ari) out of the deal. In Dickens's *The Pickwick Papers*, Arabella was Mr. Winkle's excellent new daughter-in-law.

Nicknames: Ari, Bella, Belle

Ariel: Ariel has an airy sound and aura—Shakespeare's sprite in *The Tempest* was named for the word for "air"—but it's also used for both men and women in Israel, so it sounds very grounded. And, because of the red-haired mermaid Ariel in Hans Christian Andersen's *The Little Mermaid*, the name has an extra splash of fun. (Whatever you do, don't bypass Ariel because of the plucky Disney heroine—trust me, when your Ariel is five, she'll be thrilled to be associated with the mermaid.) Ariel is also a poetic name for the city of Jerusalem.

Nickname: Ari

Auden: There is nothing inherently feminine about Auden (first syllable rhymes with "law"), but when you think about it for a little girl, the image softens and sweetens. With similarities to Autumn and Audrey, Auden is easily assimilated as a girl's name. *ER* star Noah Wyle plowed new ground

---

Cardigan Cool

Alice ✳ Beatrice ✳ Dorothy ✳ Harriet ✳ Hazel ✳ Iris
✳ Josephine ✳ Olive ✳ Opal ✳ Pearl

---

when he chose this literary surname for his daughter, introducing the notion that it could be an option for both genders. Pair Auden with an exclusively feminine middle name, such as Maria or Rose, and you have a stunning designation for your child. W. H. Auden is considered one of the greatest poets of the twentieth century, having penned such poems as "Dover," "September 1, 1939," and "Funeral Blues," which was read aloud in the film *Four Weddings and a Funeral*.

> Pair Auden with an exclusively feminine middle name, such as Maria or Rose, and you have a stunning designation for your child.

Avonlea: Warning: for Anne freaks only. Avonlea, of course, is the fictional village on Prince Edward Island where Anne of Green Gables died her hair green, broke the slate over Gilbert Blythe's head, and got Diana Barry sloshed on raspberry cordial. I've always thought it was a beautiful, romantic word, and completely suitable for a first or middle name. The *A* is soft, by the way—not like the Avon lady.

Nickname: Avon

B

Barrett: Here's a romantic find that flows easily with some of the other surnames for girls—Grier, Harper, Eliot—that have become more familiar in recent years. It's a gentle and feminine-sounding name, with a certain strength at its core, much like the great Victorian poet Elizabeth Barrett

Browning. She who wrote the words "How do I love thee? Let me count the ways" and overcame a sickly childhood and a father who refused to let her get married (she eloped in the dark of night) to become the best of the English poetesses. Her *Sonnets from the Portuguese* are just the thing for lovers to read aloud to each other.

Beatrice: Here's a button-downed name that sounds prim and proper to Yanks, but it holds far more fashion flair for our English friends across the Pond. Princess Beatrice, in all her flame-haired glory, brings a certain Fergie flashiness to her staid name. And Sir Paul McCartney's wee Bea gives the name a dusting of rock 'n' roll fairy dust. Call me crazy, but I think Beatrice will soon trot down the road Violet paved. Need more convincing? Just pop in the DVD of Emma Thompson playing the winning and likeable Beatrice in the film version of *Much Ado About Nothing*, and you may well be won over.

   Nickname: Bea

Beatrix: Anyone who likes to think about ducks and frogs and rabbits having tea parties is bound to be enchanted by Beatrix, the original name from which Beatrice was a French spin-off. Beatrix is prim with a saucy, winking side that makes it delightful on a little girl. It's the perfect name for an animal lover, if only to honor Beatrix Potter, whose Peter Rabbit books and other stories

> Anyone who likes to think about ducks and frogs and rabbits having tea parties is bound to be enchanted by Beatrix.

were based on creatures she smuggled into the house during her lonely childhood in England. (Anyone who names a duck Jemima is good in my book.)

Nickname: Bea, Trix, Trixie

Bedelia: Boys and girls alike are captivated by the zany Amelia Bedelia of the hilarious children's book series by Peggy Parish. And just where might Parish have gotten the inspiration to have her literary creation throw talcum powder all over the furniture after being told to dust, or dress the turkey by making it an outfit? Well, this derivation of Bridget has a delicious history: it was the ultimate Irish maid's name, and those cheeky servant girls were first popularly portrayed as being comically inept in the vaudeville theaters of New England in the late nineteenth century. This is a name with a yummy sense of humor, loads of cheek, and a quaint Victorian sound.

Nicknames: Beddy, Delia

Belle: It's stunning that this adorable Victorian valentine has not been reopened by today's parents, who seem to be so enamored with the hits of a hundred years ago. One-syllable sweeties Kate and Claire are very popular, while the beautiful Belle of the ball is inexplicably drinking punch in the corner, waiting for people to sign her dance card. If it doesn't seem like a "real" name because there are so many Isabelles and Anabelles out there, guess what? It's a valid full name, best used during the turn of the century and not much since. Bonus: a little Belle today will be overjoyed to share her name with the winsome heroine of *Beauty and* *the Beast.* Belle was once engaged to Ebenezer Scrooge in Dickens's *A Christmas Carol.* (No word on why the bust-up, but we can probably guess!)

Bianca: Bianca is an Italian name that has been so well used by parents of Anglo, Latina, and African American heritage that it no longer seems particularly Italian. (If you're looking for a Boot-inspired name, see Francesca and Ginevra.) Bianca has spunk, attitude, and a fashionista sheen, possibly due to Mick Jagger's socialite ex, Bianca Jagger. It doesn't seem to yield an obvious nickname, though on *All My Children* the Bianca character is sometimes called "Bic," which is cute. Bianca was Cassio's mistress in Shakespeare's *Othello.*

   Nickname: Bic

Blanche: Once upon a time, this was a fancy French import, chosen to impart some va-va-voom on the baby girls of the new twentieth century. Many names from that era are making fashionable comebacks, but Blanche sounds kind of hardened and blowsy, not unlike Blanche DuBois, Tennessee Williams's female lead in *A Streetcar Named Desire.* (Keep in mind that this character also ends up drunk and in the looney bin.)

Blue: If you want to do something kind of wild and adventurous for your baby's middle name slot, check out Blue. This cool color name is also a big celebrity favorite: several star babies have it as a middle name (John Travolta and Kelly Preston spelled it Bleu to act all French), and some even have this hued hottie as a first name (U2's The Edge named his daughter Blue Angel). Oh, and we must not forget the Spice Girls and their variegated contributions to the baby-name pantheon: Geri "Ginger Spice" Halliwell has a baby Bluebell. But assuming you're not a Spice Girl or a member of a world famous rock outfit of any kind, you can bring Blue down to the realm of mere mortals and use it as a middle name. Our literary connection, however, Blue Balliet, goes about life and writing (she wrote the children's best seller *Chasing Vermeer*) with this most artistic and vibrant name in the prime slot.

If you like Briana, see fellow unlikely lit hits Olivia, Jessica, and Chloe.

Briana: Could a name sound more made-up than Briana? Well, it actually was made up, but not by baby namers in the 1990s. Edmund Spenser himself cooked up Briana for his epic poem *The Faerie Queene*, which just goes to show you never know which unlikely names have august literary depths (see also Vanessa and Jessica). Briana is a blockbuster in every spelling, so you would certainly resign your little girl to a life shared with many other Brianas, but if that doesn't phase you, go for it. At least it has classic roots, unlike, say, Kaylee.

Brontë: This is a name with all the literary élan in the world, immediately identified with the three writing sisters Charlotte (*Jane Eyre*), Emily (*Wuthering Heights*), and Anne (*Agnes Grey*). They were daughters of a clergyman and wrote vividly of the Yorkshire moors, where they grew up. As a first name, Brontë is bold and strong, but softened by the romantic image of those three sisters in Empire-waist gowns, concocting sagas by lamplight.

C

Carrie: Carrie was a huge homesteader hit, and the name of Half Pint's little sister in Laura Ingalls Wilder's prairie stories, so it's no wonder the name still wears calico and churns butter. The only problem is, people cozied up to Carrie all through the last century, and with another peak spiking as recently as the seventies, it now belongs to quite a few minivan-driving moms. Still cute and sweet, Carrie could be used as an abbreviation for Caroline, as it was in the Ingalls family. (Caroline is a rising classic; it's always in the top 100.)

Carson: Carson is crisp, coolly elegant, and not in the top 1,000 for girls, making it a vividly literary and unique choice. Yes, the relatives will complain that it sounds like a boy's name (a boys' top 100 name at that!), but hopefully you can calm them down with references to Carson McCullers, the name's most famous bearer *and* a woman. McCullers was born Lula Carson Smith in Georgia, and went on to become one of the most revered writers of the

---

Dishy Irish Dames

Aine ❖ Deirdre ❖ Eudora ❖ Isolde ❖ Niamh

Southern gothic genre. She is most well known for *The Heart Is a Lonely Hunter* and *The Member of the Wedding*.

Nickname: Carsie

Catriona: If you like the Gaelic step-dancing sound of Caitlin, but are (justifiably) worried that it's too trendy, do consider Catriona, a Scottish name that wears a tartan skirt and plays the bagpipes. Pronounced "Cat-TRAIN-a," or phonetically if you choose, Catriona is a cheerful throwback and a wonderful name to pair especially with MacGregor or MacIntosh or those sorts of Scotch beauties. (Olympic gold medalist speedskater Catriona LeMay Doan adds a sporty note to the name.) Catriona MacGregor Drummond was the beautiful title character of Robert Louis Stevenson's novel *Catriona*, a sequel to *Kidnapped*.

Nickname: Cat

Celia/Celie/Cecelia: Celia is a gem just waiting to be picked by parents who value the classics and the arts. This name is feminine without being froufrou and sounds polished without being stuck up. What is distinctive about the Bard's Celia of *As You Like It*? Her wonderful way as a friend. She is cousin Rosalind's cool-headed advisor in love and her brave defender, challenging her own father when the Duke accuses Rosalind of being a traitor. Baby namers attracted to the newly stylish century names—Emma, Grace, Claire, et al., which reigned a hundred years ago and are being dusted off for new-millennium girls—will find a rarely used alternative in coolly beautiful Celia.

Celie was the core character in Alice Walker's *The Color Purple*, and could therefore make a vivid choice. **Cecilia**

enlarges on the theme and adds a musical note: Saint Cecelia is the patron saint of music. There is a character named Cecelia Brady in *The Love of the Last Tycoon* by F. Scott Fitzgerald.

Charlotte: Charlotte Brontë was the Yorkshire novelist and poet who won a million hearts with her enduring *Jane Eyre*. Her name carries on as well, with a measure of the poise, grace, and spirit that Ms. Brontë possessed. Like her lit namesake, Charlotte is outwardly decorous but also very romantic at the core. There's also a lingering Jane Austen aura as well: Charlotte Lucas was a pivotal character in *Pride and Prejudice*. Like Oliver, Jasper, Phoebe, and Louisa, Charlotte is gaining new admirers who love very old names that have aged beautifully and sound somehow innovative today. Bonus: Hopefully after reading E. B. White's *Charlotte's Web* to your young Charlotte, she won't be afraid of spiders, but instead consider them kindred spirits.

Like Chloe? So does your neighbor! Consider Phoebe, Clio, and Daphne as zippier ancient Greek names.

Chloe: This just goes to show you never know which faddish-sounding names actually have lengthy and interesting histories. Check this out: Seventeenth-century Puritans, who refused to dub their daughters with any Catholic or Anglican saints' names, scoured the New Testament for new options and unearthed a passing reference to a Chloe in 1 Corinthians 1:11. Soon Pilgrim playgroups had wee Chloes running around, no doubt the lives of the party among their playmates Prudence and Resolved. A little after New Testament times, in the second century AD, Greek novelist Longus penned the enduring romantic tale of *Daphnis and Chloe*.

Clara/Clarinda: Clara, like Bella, Lila, and Eva, is an heirloom name that hasn't been done to death (see Emma). Wildly popular during Queen Victoria's era, Clara cooled down for almost a century, at which point it started to slowly ascend. The French Claire is a top 100 hit, and many people see it as an alternative to Kate. (Three mothers-to-be I know waffled between Kate and Claire, with two choosing Kate and pining thereafter for Claire.)

If you like Clara, see Ella, Julia, and Nora.

But between Claire and Clara, the latter is more distinctive at this point, and it also has a wonderful connection to *The Nutcracker*, Tchaikovsky's ballet suite that revolves around a German girl named Clara Stahlbaum. Of course, it must be said that in the original book, *The Nutcracker and the Mouse King* by E. T. A. Hoffmann, the girl is called Marie, while Clara—or Klärchen—is the name of one of her dolls. Still, many book versions today use the name from the ballet. Actor Ewan McGregor named his daughter Clara.

Clarinda: It might sound like this is just Clara with frills, but Clarinda has a golden literary lineage: Edmund Spenser invented this name in his epic poem *The Faerie Queene*. Two centuries later, Robert Burns trotted it out in his "Verses to Clarinda." Burns rapturously called her "Fair Empress of the Poet's Soul."

Clarissa: This Italian form of Clara is as froufrou as other names ending in *issa*, and by and large, those ultra-lacy doilies are being replaced by sturdier appellations (although Alyssa and Marissa are still very popular). But this name's literary connection offsets its otherwise dainty connotation: Clarissa was the first name of the ill-fated Mrs. Dalloway in Virginia Woolf's classic *Mrs. Dalloway*.

> If you like Clarissa, consider equally feminine Ophelia or Francesca.

Clio: Shuffle the letters a little bit and you'd almost have Chloe. Instead, you have Clio, which has the same vivacious sound with a more futuristic edge. Plus, unlike the overused Chloe, it hasn't even touched the top 1,000. In Greek mythology, Clio is the muse of poetry and history. As such, she is often depicted with a scroll or a set of tablets, which is how she is shown in the sumptuous Vermeer artwork called *The Allegory of Painting*. With Clio, you have a more artsy, quirky, and infinitely more singular name than trendy Chloe.

Clover: The greenhouse blooms—Lily, Violet, Daisy—are getting all the buzz, but what about wildflowers such as Clover? This is a cheery, sunshine-infused name that suggests open fields, blue skies, and scented meadows. It's homey, innocent, old-fashioned, and sweet as pie. It's a true find for those on the prowl for something peerless for their peerless darling. Clover Carr lived up to her name's sunny disposition with a personality to match as the pretty, clever, and much-loved sister of Katy Carr in the 1860s children's classic *What Katy Did* by Susan Coolidge.

Nickname: Clo or Clove

Colette/Cosette: Both Colette and Cosette are flirty French names with significant literary foundations. Neither one has been used all that much in North America (although Colette saw some action in the fifties and sixties), so both would make novel, vibrant choices. **Colette** was the pen name of the French novelist Sidonie-Gabrielle Colette. She was a music hall performer at the Moulin Rouge (doesn't that sound about right?) and author of the Claudine series. Euphrasie "Cosette" Fauchelevent was Victor Hugo's sweet waif who grows up to fall in love with Marius Pontmercy in *Les Misérables*.

> Both Colette and Cosette are flirty French names with significant literary foundations.

Cordelia: When Anne of Green Gables first met Marilla Cuthbert, the starchy spinster who would become like a mother to her, she tried to shed her real first name: "I would love to be called Cordelia," she said. "It's such a perfectly elegant name." Of course, that didn't fly with Marilla, but the name Cordelia will always have a soft spot in the hearts of Anne fans. It's also the name of King Lear's loyal daughter, although her name has never touched the popularity of her nasty sister Regan. What a shame, because Cordelia is so polished, romantic, and—Anne said it—"perfectly elegant." Be the first to revive this ladylike beauty and everyone else will marvel at your taste.

Nickname: Delia, Cordie

Cressida: This golden name is almost wholly British in use, which is too bad, because it's so pretty and unusual. In fact, there's nothing like it on our side of the ocean, which makes Cressida ripe for the picking for parents on a quest for a rare and exotic find. In literature, Cressida has a sterling pedigree. She appears in many medieval and Renaissance retellings of the story of the Trojan War as a woman of Troy who falls in love with King Prium's son, Troilus. Her story unfolds in Chaucer's poem "Troilus and Cressida," and Shakespeare's play, also called *Troilus and Cressida*.

D

Daisy: Bright, sunshiny Daisy is just waiting to be plucked. (I couldn't resist.) Seriously, who doesn't like daisies? And flower names are white hot. (Think Violet and Lily.) More cheerful than Rose, and more accessible than Iris or Poppy, this is a hit waiting to happen. (In England, this darling is in the top 25.) Bookworms know that the main Daisies— Daisy Miller, the title character of Henry James's novella, and Daisy Buchanan, the Paris Hilton–like lady from *The Great Gatsby*—both met bleak endings, But the name is still lovely, quaint, and ebullient. Meg Ryan's baby daughter from China is Daisy True.

> More cheerful than Rose, and more accessible than Iris or Poppy, Daisy is a hit waiting to happen.

Daphne: Daphne is enchanting, soft, and smart-sounding. It's quite amazing this mythological name hasn't been used more commonly outside of England, because as fabulous as it is, Daphne has yet to break into the top 500 in the U.S. It shares an ageless Greek beauty with Phoebe and Chloe. The Greek myth goes that the nymph Daphne shapeshifted into a laurel tree to escape Apollo, who chased her incessantly. Dame Daphne du Maurier wrote the short story "The Birds" and the novel *Rebecca*, both made into films by Alfred Hitchcock.

Darby/Dagny: Darby, like Toby and Colby, are bouncy, peppy names that sound equally cute on a boy or a girl. Pairing Darby, which positively effervesces, with a feminine standard such as Rose or Grace or Jane, makes for an appealing package. Like other gender benders that cross over easily to the girls' side, Darby also has loads of freckle-faced, tea-party-in-the-tree-house allure. In Herminie Templeton Kavanagh's *Darby O'Gill and the Good People*, Darby was a man, but don't let that stop you. And if you happen to have a big Irish last name—like O'Gill—how can you possibly resist? (I've also heard Dabny for girls, which is equally darling.) More polished and European sounding, **Dagny** is a Scandinavian girl's name, heard in the form of Dagny Taggart, a no-nonsense railroad executive in Ayn Rand's magnum opus *Atlas Shrugged*.

Darcy: Which reader of *Pride and Prejudice* is not forever and always in love with Mr. Darcy? Though his surname was used as a boy's name mainly in the sixties and seventies, it's tilted over to the girls' side now. Even so, Darcy is a bit dated, despite its bouncy Irish sound and connection to the guy who made us all go weak in the knees with "the violence of his affection" for Lizzie.

Deirdre: Here's an Irish old-timer that most people can pronounce and spell without too much trouble. Missing from the top 1,000 for almost twenty years, Deirdre could sound new again, if not as freshly minted as upstarts Niamh, Fiona, and Maeve. Deirdre is the principal tragic heroine in Irish mythology. There are three plays based on her story, including William Butler Yeats's *Deirdre* (1907).

Love Emma? Who doesn't? Bypass mass popularity with the equally charming Delia, Louisa, or Clara.

Delia: Delia is alluring and winsome, pretty without the extra frills of some of today's excessive exotics. It should appeal to parents in search of something antique (Delia was a Victorian hit) yet not overdone like revivals Emma, Isabella, or Sophia. Delia is just as lovely, but rarely used. Delia was a character in Sir Philip Sydney's epic poem *The Arcadia*.

Diana: This is a nice-looking name that somehow lost its luster, despite being forever and always linked to the beautiful Princess Diana. Popular between the 1940s and the 1980s, Diana has only just recently slipped off the top 100. I predict it will slip further until a possible Diana revival in 2040, about one hundred years after its last lustrous run at the top. Diana was Apollo's twin sister. In Roman mythology she is known as the goddess of the hunt and the moon. Anne of Green Gables devotees know that Diana Barry was her very own "kindred spirit."

Dominique: A decorative name with a French finesse, Dominique spiked in the ornamental nineties, then began its plummet southward. It still has a certain *je ne sais quois*, but fresher Francophones with more flair include Elodie, Amelie, Delphine, and Mignon. Dominique Francon is Howard Roark's love interest and a main character in Ayn Rand's *The Fountainhead*.

Doone: Celebrities have almost as much influence over middle names as they do first names, and right now the stars are cultivating new ground in that all-important intermediate slot. Exhibit A: Tallulah Pine Le Bon (Duran Duran's Simon). Exhibit B: Talula Fyfe Dempsey (Patrick of *Grey's Anatomy*). Exhibit C: Daisy True Ryan (Meg is her mommy). Pine, Fyfe, and True are all compact, jazzy, and wildly creative, and they are all in the middle, the perfect spot for such naming audacity. Which leads me to Doone, a jewel of a name that evokes a breezy feeling of windy moors and sandy dunes. *Lorna Doone: A Romance of Exmoor*, was

---

Singular Sensations

Auden ✻ Avonlea ✻ Barrett ✻ Brontë ✻ Gaia ✻ Jerusha ✻ Marlowe ✻ Odessa ✻ Owen ✻ Quintana

---

written by Richard Doddridge Blackmore in 1869, but at this point, Doone has more currency than Lorna. Lorna Doone, by the way, was a beautiful heiress who fell in love with a humble farmer and who fought valiantly to be able to marry him.

Dorothy: Some ninety years ago, Dorothy was at the crest of the baby name list, topped only by Mary in the number 1 spot. Readers of the Oz books (*The Wonderful Wizard of Oz* came out in 1900) were enthralled with spunky Princess Dorothy of Oz and her ruby red shoes. After that kind of fanfare, things cooled down a lot for Dorothy, and now she sounds like someone's grandma, which, in baby name terms, is a good thing. Dorothy is quaint and sweet, but due to Dorothy Gale's numerous capers in Oz, still has an adventuresome spirit. This would be a perfect sister name for Alice, because both are beloved children's book heroines who were swept away to alternative worlds. Doro is a cool reduction.

Nickname: Doro, Dot, Dottie

Dylan: Oh, I know this is a top 20 boy's name, but it sounds miles fresher and more sparkly for the girls. (I can just hear some husbands muttering, "What's next? Frank, Mike, and Dave for girls?") Like Ryan, Peyton, and Morgan, Dylan has the goods to make a dent in the girls' lists, too. Why? It *is* a soft, poetic name, due to the influence of Welsh poet Thomas and his self-appointed namesake, Bob Dylan. And a nine-year-old Dylan I know pulls it off with spunk, tomboyish cutes, and real femininity. Dylan sounds like the kind of girl who might play hockey, but also sketches fashion designs in her spare time.

 E

Echo: This is a name with a ring to it, for more reasons than one. Echo, though known chiefly as a sound you hear after bellowing into the Grand Canyon, is a genuine girl's name that dates back to ancient Greece. In modern-day Des Moines, say, it would probably be prudent to stick with this as a middle name, where you can get your yah yahs out in a harmless fashion. In Ovid's version of Echo's story, our nymph with the lovely voice caught the attention of Zeus, but unfortunately received the wrath of his jealous wife. Her punishment? Echo could never say anything again except for the last words of other people's sentences.

Looking for a super-creative and richly evocative middle name? Check out Echo, a valid girl's name that dates back centuries, with a cool legend attached to it.

Edith: With this cameo-brooch name, you have to hope for a daughter who is either so quirky she turns it inside out, or so creatively gifted that she infuses great gusts of color and drama (good drama) into it. I happen to know a theatrical young lady in the latter category, so the name is growing on me. But when I'm just thinking about the name itself, borne handsomely by American novelist Edith Wharton, I still see doilies and fussy wallpaper. And to be honest, I still hear Edith Bunker screeching Archie's name. Edie's cute, though.

Nickname: Edie

Elena: The faintly gilded veneer of this old Russian and Spanish form of Helen has attracted a surprising number of parents. Elena is pretty, old-fashioned, and has just a pinch of the exotic to keep things interesting. Elena Kuragina is Pierre's high-society wife in *War and Peace* by Leo Tolstoy.

Elinor: Pop quiz: What country does the august Elinor come from? It sounds British, but actually it's the French spin on Helen. It was brought to English ears in the twelfth century by French queen Eleanor of Aquitaine, one of the most powerful women in the middle ages. A hit in the 1920s, Elinor has been absent from the top 1,000 for almost sixty years, which means it's all yours if you're after a brainy name with substance and dignity. In keeping with her name, Elinor Dashwood is reserved, practical, and thoughtful, and is therefore the "sense" in Jane Austen's *Sense and Sensibility*.

Nickname: Ellie

Elise: If you're searching for a more creative way to honor a beloved Elizabeth (my grandma's name and quite possibly your grandma's name, too!), the French miniature Elise may hold appeal. Certainly, many parents in the last century have been drawn to Elise's subdued loveliness and lyrical grace: the name has never fallen out of favor, nor has it worn out its welcome. It's a classic that gently shimmers with style. *Für Elise* is Ludwig van Beethoven's shimmering piano classic, which enhances the name even more. In literature, Elise appears as a character in *The Miser* by Molière.

Elizabeth/Liesl/Lizzie/Elsa/Eliza: Elizabeth is one of the grand dames of baby names, a biblical, queenly appellation that has weathered some two thousand years of history and still sounds splendid. The coolest thing about Elizabeth is the huge buffet of nickname choices you can select from to make this classic your own. Lisa, Liz, and Beth are definitely out the style window, but Ellie, Libby, Lizzie, Bess, and Lilabet (the pet name for the current Queen of England) all sound fresh and distinctive. The German form **Liesl** (a *Sound of Music* name), the Scottish Elsbeth, and the Swedish **Elsa** (the lion in *Born Free*) are all magnificent ways to make Elizabeth international. **Eliza** is my favorite pod from the Mother Name Ship. It sounds modern and antique at the same time, and is as adorable, stylish, and feisty as Eliza Doolittle of *Pygmalion* fame. Plus, Eliza, though catching the coattails of the Emma/Isabella rage just slightly, is far less used than Elizabeth. It's hard to think of a name that hits the style sweet spot—not too common but not odd—so fabulously. This is a true winner. By the way, Elizabeth Bennett of *Pride and Prejudice* went by Elizabeth, Eliza, and (mostly) **Lizzie**.

Nicknames: Lisa, Liz, Beth, Biz, Ellie, Libby, Lizzie, Bess, Lilabet

Ella: Almost inevitably, gorgeous Ella has catapulted into the dizzying heights of

Ella is overheating. Instead, nab Clara, Julia, and Nora, which are just warming up.

the top 15, definitely on the coattails of Emma and Emily, and much to the chagrin of baby namers who really wanted to pick something distinctive. The bittersweet news for them is that Ella *is* distinctive, polished, intelligent, lovely, but it's no longer original. Some minty-fresh choices at this point might include Eliana, Eliza, and Elle, with the latter providing an almost Ella sound in a sleeker, *far* less popular presentation. Ella Lorena Kennedy was Scarlett O'Hara's daughter with Frank Kennedy in *Gone With the Wind*.

Ellis: My husband had a great-aunt named Alice Ellis, and when he was little he thought her first and last name were the same. Almost, but not quite. Alice is a cardigan-cool, retro-chic lady who just evolved from old-lady-with-doilies-on-her-chairs to a little hipster. Ellis, on the other hand, is crisp, snazzy, and wearing a fabulous linen pant designed by Michael Kors; she's thoroughly modern. And here's the best part: Emily Brontë originally published *Wuthering Heights* under the pseudonym Ellis Bell. A girl named Ellis just seems destined for great things.

If you like Emily, bypass Ella and Emma (both are everywhere already) and bear in mind Esmé, Emerson, Emmaline, or Emilia, the lovely Italian shape of Emily, found in no fewer than four Shakespearean plays.

Emily/Emilia: What can be said about Emily that hasn't already been echoed a million times by parents around the world who love this name? Not much. Emily charms, brightens, and lures baby namers who, though they know it's the number one girl's name, can't resist anyway. The result is classes with two or three Emilys, college roommates both named Emily, and no doubt, down the road, clubs of Emilys (much like the groups formed by people with hypercommon names such as Bob). Ah, but even though it's the next Mary or Linda or Jennifer, Emily continues to be chosen by parents of all stripes, especially well-educated ones who appreciate the name's significant literary ties: Emily Jane Brontë wrote *Wuthering Heights*, and Emily Elizabeth Dickenson penned reams of quintessential poetry—more than seventeen hundred poems in all.

Emma: Emma has catapulted in the past decade to the number 1 spot on the girl's list, propelled by qualities modern parents appreciate: it's sweet, straightforward, and easy to spell. A top 10 hit a hundred years ago, it may be one of the only names to come full circle in popularity, as it's now experiencing what's sure to be a long-term revival. The only problem is that, well, everyone loves it to pieces, so if originality is your aim, bypass Queen Emma and consider Esmé, Ellery, or even Emmaline if you can't quite let go completely. *Emma* was Jane Austen's beloved 1816 comic novel.

E is for Emma, and also Esmé, Ellery, or Emmaline.

Esmé: Think of emerging from your great-grandmother's attic, just having found an exotic and lovely heirloom somehow no one else had unearthed previously. This is the sentimental, distinctive, and altogether wonderful feeling the name Esmé carries. The French shortened Esmerelda a couple of centuries ago and Esmé caught on as its own entity. Meaning "beloved," Esmé is the star of a cherished short story by J. D. Salinger. In "For Esmé—with Love and Squalor," a precocious young girl in an English tearoom during World War II enchants an American soldier. When Esmé discovers her new acquaintance is a writer, she solemnly requests a custom-written story for her, preferably one "full of squalor...I'm terribly interested in squalor." This rarest of names sounds accessible due to sharing qualities with chart toppers Emily and Emma. Celeb trailblazers include Michael J. Fox and Tracy Pollan, whose fourth child is Esmé.

Estella: When people say, "Isn't Estella an old lady's name?" you can respond by saying, "Yes! That's exactly the point." Estella does sound rather creaky and fusty, just the kind of name some intrepid baby namer can blow the dust off of and use with smashing results for a baby girl. Estella has tons more vigor and charisma than Estelle, too. It's romantic and beautiful, like Estella of Dickens's *Great Expectations*.

   Nicknames: Estie, Ella, Stella

Esther: Esther (the Persian form of Hadassah—don't ask me to explain *that* one) is one of the magnificent heroines of the Bible, the stunning queen of Persia who saved her Jewish people from a genocidal plot. To this day Jews celebrate her tact and valor on the holiday of Purim. Despite this exotic history, it still might sound a bit plain and outmoded to you. But wait! Its old-lady-cardigan days are numbered—hipsters such as Ewan McGregor have started using it. Esther was a character in Dickens's *Bleak House*.

Eudora: Melodious Eudora has a Southern accent and an Irish twinkle. It's a lit heroine name that is clearly such, and conveys intelligence, charm, and creative ability. It would make a splendid choice for parents on a quest for a rare antique. Eudora Welty wrote with sublime skill about her home state of Mississippi in short-story collections such as *A Curtain of Green*. Her novel *The Optimist's Daughter* won the Pulitzer Prize for fiction in 1972.

Evangeline: A gorgeously literary and sorely neglected name, Evangeline is on the cusp of rediscovery. *Lost* star Evangeline Lilly puts a beautiful young face on an old gem. This little star has that offbeat, innovative quality that appeals to creative people. (Lately I've heard it attached to the baby daughter of singer-songwriters, which seems about right.) "Evangeline: A Tale of Acadie" is a poem by Henry Wadsworth Longfellow.

Nicknames: Evie, Vangie

Fanny: Fanny Brawne may have been the inamorata of poet John Keats, but few people in our culture would be enamored with her first name. A diminutive of Frances, Fanny was used in various Dickens and Austen novels. It's also another word for toukis, which disqualifies it as a given name for the time being.

Fern: If your husband immediately shuts you down with a dismissive, "Fern? Like that plant in the corner?," raise your chin proudly and tell him botanical names are the height of fashion and, furthermore, that the plant in the corner is a succulent. Fern evokes a leafy, green sensibility and shares one-syllable sleekness with Pearl, Grace, Jane, and Anne. It also has tons of Victorian charm, and a gently stylish air. And I'm only now getting to the best part: Fern is the sweet, plucky little farm girl who stands up for Wilbur the pig in the beloved children's chestnut *Charlotte's Web*. Your Fern will love being named after such a worthy heroine.

Flannery: Flannery is one of the most recognizably literary names you could give your child, because almost everyone associates it with Flannery O'Connor, the queen of Southern gothic fiction. It's Irish, lyrical, and absolutely infused with bookish élan. Still, Flannery isn't snooty, it's just intertwined with the image of O'Connor and her peacocks, writing the novels and short stories that would one day shock and provoke generations of readers. If you're looking for something very distinctive and singular, Flannery is warm, lovely, and as close to peerless as you can get.

> Flannery's Irish, lyrical, and absolutely infused with bookish élan.

Fleur: You can hardly pick a more dreamy, lushly romantic name than Fleur, which is French for "flower." John Galsworthy must have thought so when he named one of his young heroines Fleur in the literary-though-soapy *Forsyte*

Saga. The problem with using any French word as a first name is that it can sound a little too chichi, especially if your heritage is nowhere close to being French. My advice is to follow that great baby namer Angelina Jolie's lead and infuse the whole package with some French flair as she did by giving baby Shiloh the middle name Nouvel ("new"). Fleur as a middle name? C'est magnifique.

Flora: If the blooming décor, gingerbread trim, and rose-colored sensibility of the Victorian era were distilled into a name, it would be Flora. This ultraromantic name pulls off great sweetness and femininity without being foofy. It goes smashingly well with the flower name trend—Violet, Lily, Daisy, etc.—but sounds even fresher and more verdant. All of the spring fever the name evokes dates back to Flora, the goddess of flowers and springtime in Roman mythology.

Florence: Florence Nightingale single-handedly turned the name of her birthplace in Italy into a Victorian blockbuster hit. That was about 120 years ago now, the same time period when current favorites Violet, Lillian, and Emma flourished. Florence is just begging to be dusted off by a couple of visionaries who can see its quaintness. The Florence, Italy, connection is a good one, too; it enhances the name with pictures of that sumptuous city, one of the world's most beautiful. Bonus: Just ask a French person to pronounce it and you might be sold on the spot. Flo is a kicky little nickname. In *Little Women*, Florence was the March girls' cousin.

Nickname: Flo

Frances/Francie: There are those who would disagree with me, but Frances is a loveable name on all counts. You could call her Franny (how cute is that?), Francie, or France, or you could even call her Frances if you like, and I do. Actress Amanda Peet concurs, having named her baby Frances Pen (after her mother Penny). It's more World War I than Victorian and less flowery than some of those revivals with *a* endings; I predict Frances could rise in the future, alongside Violet and Alice, but she'll never approach Ava status, thank goodness. Frances Hodgson Burnett wrote the enduring novels *The Secret Garden* and *A Little Princess*, and there is a series of perfectly adorable children's classics starring a badger named Frances. **Francie** adds a flirty flounce to the Frances model, and could be used as an everyday nickname for a Frances. Francie was the beloved young heroine at the center of Betty Smith's *A Tree Grows in Brooklyn*.

Nicknames: Franny, Francie, France

Are you charmed by quaint, turn-of-the-century names such as Ava, Violet, and Claire? Fashionable Frances is just as picturesque.

Francesca/Frankie: If you have any Italian blood in you whatsoever—or maybe you just love all things from the Boot—consider this most delectable name, as opulent and vibrant as Venetian glass or paper art from Florence. Francesca manages to be supremely feminine without being froufrou. The "chesca" sound, so vivacious and energetic, adds some fun cha-cha-cha. **Frankie** is darling for a little sassy pants, too. (Think of the winsome heroine of Carson McCullers's

The Member of the Wedding.) Francesca was a character in Shakespeare's *Measure for Measure*.

Freya: What do Freya and Brianna have in common? Both are number 23 on the popularity charts, Freya in England and Brianna here. *Freya?* We haven't even heard of it in these parts, which is fantastic for those who freak out if any of their shortlisted names have even flirted with the top 1,000. Freya actually has a long and illustrious history, beginning with Freya, the Norse goddess of fertility and love. (Her Greek counterparts are Venus and Aphrodite.) Our Friday was taken from Freyja Day. A very pretty, extremely unusual choice.

❦ G ❦

Gabriela: This name has quickly ascended over the past twenty years to become a top 60 name, and it probably won't stop until it's firmly entrenched in the top 20. Why? Gabriela is breathtaking, a spirited, strong, and aesthetically beautiful name; plus, Gabby and Brie are adorable nicknames. But...Gabriela is starting to feel like Isabella, Alyssa, or Brianna: lovely sounding yet trendy and overused. Think about Genevieve, Graciela, or Francesca for ornate, feminine names that have plenty of mileage left. Gabriela Mistral was a Chilean poet who was

> Gabriela's gorgeous, but so are Francesca and Ginevra.

the first Latin American to win the Nobel Prize for literature in 1945.

Nicknames: Gabby, Brie

Gaia: Before Emma Thompson dusted this earthy beauty off a few years ago, you may have only heard Gaia ("GUY-a") attached to some vegetarian restaurants here and there. In English class, though, you possibly took notice of Gaia in conjunction with the Greek myths. She was the wife of Uranus, the mother of the Titans (remember them?), and the goddess of the earth, hence all the gardening and nature evocations. This true iconoclast is well-suited for a child who gobbles palak paneer as her hot-dog-munching playgroup stares in fascination.

Garnet: Garnet peaked in the 1910s, when gemstones such as Pearl, Opal, and Ruby were at their shiniest. Garnet has a few features that her bejeweled sisters don't, namely a tomboyish surname sound that dovetails perfectly with what's hot now. If you do unearth this treasure, know that you have really done some excavation: Garnet hasn't cracked the top 1,000 since the 1930s. In *Thimble Summer*, the 1939 Newbery Medal–winning novel by Elizabeth Enright, nine-year-old Garnet Linden finds a silver thimble in a dried-up riverbed near her family's farm. She comes to believe the thimble has magical powers as her family's fortunes begin to reverse.

Georgiana: With the upswing of George on the boys' side, it won't be long before the feminizations start to sparkle again. Georgia is already a hot name in some pockets of the country, but what about her regal and graceful neighbor

Georgiana (pronounced "George-AY-na" or "Georgie-Anna")? The luxurious name is saved from decadence by the near-irresistible nickname **Georgie**. Georgiana was the much-loved little sister of Mr. Darcy in *Pride and Prejudice*.

Nickname: Georgie

> Georgiana was the much-loved little sister of Mr. Darcy in *Pride and Prejudice*.

Gertrude: Let's begin the tally on the positive side, why don't we? Gertrude was a saint—Gertrude the Great, no less—and the name of the American writer Gertrude Stein. At the turn of the century, the name Gertrude was so ridiculously well liked it was today's Emily or Gabrielle—something you would call your daughter if you wanted her to be popular. Times have changed, and now saddling a baby with this Teutonic clunker would be ill-advised, unless you have a stellar reason, like naming her after a beloved family member, perhaps. (You might want to tattoo the words "named for Grandmother" on her forehead, too.) Sister names might include Krimhilda and Hermantrude.

Ginevra: If you've examined Gabriella and found it to be too popular, here's a sumptuous G name infused with Italianate beauty. Ginevra, somewhat similar to Genevieve, gives you the basic "Jen" sound that people are so nuts about and yields at least four nicknames (Gin, Ginny, Nev, Evra). This is the Italian spin on Guinevere, the legendary queen consort of King Arthur.

Nicknames: Gin, Ginny, Nev, Evra

Grace: This virtuous name shines with loveliness, sophistication, benevolence, and purity, a fact that has not escaped the attention of untold baby namers, who have collectively hurled it into the top 20. Grace is so irresistible that I could probably offer you a trip to Maui and a TV makeover if you picked another meritorious name—think Ruth, Mercy, or Verity—and chances are, you'd still go for Grace. The pick is completely widespread at this point, so you might consider Hope or Faith, which are quite a bit less popular. (Hope's not even on the top 100!) Grace was Samuel's wife in John Bunyan's *The Pilgrim's Progress*.

Gretel/Greta: Ahh, a fairy-tale name, belonging to the young heroine of one of the most illustrious and oft-told stories of the Brothers Grimm. Gretel, along with her brother Hansel, was almost baked in an oven by a witch (who was subsequently rotisseried by Gretel). After Gretel prevails, she returns via the breadcrumb path to her father. "Then all anxiety was at an end," the tale winds up, "and they lived together in perfect happiness." Okay, so the whole baking-a-person aspect is a little, well, grim. But sometimes, a girl's gotta do what a girl's gotta do; they did have a happy ending, didn't they? Gretel is a pretty, quaint German strudel of a name. (Those are in short supply.) An abbreviation of Margaret, it could very well be imported in larger measure as parents are choosing all kinds of ethnic tribute names. Sister name **Greta**, with the popular *a* ending similar to superstars Isabella or Emma, may be a more engaging alternative (and more to the point, it doesn't have any "baking" baggage).

Guinevere: This name conjures up a medieval tapestry of rich and romantic evocations, chiefly Camelot and the Knights of the Round Table. Guinevere was married to King Arthur, but loved Lancelot. Their affair precipitated all kinds of battles and bloodshed and is one of the best-known tragic love stories of all time. Guinevere is actually an old form of Jennifer; the high-drama genuine article is not only infinitely more striking and fascinating, but original. Gwyn is a user-friendly way to shorten it.

Nickname: Gwyn

> **A B C**
>
> Go really old school with **Guinevere**, the medieval form of Jennifer.

Gwendolyn: This Welsh stalwart was last semipopular in the fifties, so it may be a tad soon for a resurgence. Still, close cousin Gwyneth has been spotted in the most stylish circles, so perhaps Gwendolyn could piggyback on its coattails. Whether it's in vogue or not won't matter to those who wish to honor Gwendolyn Brooks, the revered poet who died at age eighty-three in 2000 with, it is said, a pen in her hand. She was the first African American to win the Pulitzer Prize for poetry ("Annie Allen").

Nickname: Gwen

H

Hannah: Just a short twenty years ago or so, Hannah was a mostly Jewish name that seemed too plain and soft for the decorative eighties. Was it Woody Allen's *Hannah and Her Sisters* that sparked the quiet Hannah revolution? Who knows, but this gentle name sky-rocketed from rare usage to a zenith of popularity, reaching number 2 a few years ago. It's the kind of name people love so much that they use it in spite of the fact that there is a log-jam of Hannahs out there already. It's sweet yet strong, old-fashioned but modern. When you get right down to it, that's the combination most people want. Trivia: Hannah is one of only a handful of palindrome names, if that floats your boat. (See also Otto.) You might also like Harper and Honoria, if you're really after an *H* name. Hannah Mullet was the March family's maid in *Little Women*.

> There is a logjam of Hannah's out there already, so avoid the traffic and consider Harper and Honoria.

Harper: Like Flannery, Harper is a literary name that reso-nates as such, and although the former has never cracked the top 1,000, the latter has broken through and is rising slowly. (I do mean *slowly*, so don't worry about it becoming trendy.) Harper is elegant, confident, and imbued with a slightly quirky, Southern accent. If only the rarest treasures will do for your little girl, put Harper on your short list, along with fellow Southern tomboys Eliot and Flannery. Pair it with Maria or Lilianna, some kind of lushly feminine name, for a presentation at the height of style. Harper Lee is the author of *To Kill a Mockingbird*.

Harriet: This grand old dame is so outmoded and musty it is absolutely perfect for parents looking to unearth something truly peerless for their daughter. (Peerless here, but not in England, where this stylin' oldie is number 80.) It's got funk, whimsy, and, best of all, very few are bold enough to use it. Hattie is an adorable derivation if you feel a two-year-old can't quite handle Harriet in all its glory, but you may be surprised: This name has been borne by all kinds of literary heroines in books from *Emma* to *Harriet the Spy*. Both Harriet Jacobs and Harriet Beecher Stowe were writers and abolitionists; the latter authored *Uncle Tom's Cabin*.

Nickname: Hattie

Hazel: Here is your chance to get in on the grassroots level of an old-fashioned baby-name revival, à la Violet and Lillian. Hazel was a top 25 name a hundred years ago, and some baby-name watchers, including me, have been waiting for it to take off again for several years. Julia Roberts surely gave the name a helping hand when she bestowed it on her baby girl twin. Do focus on the botanical (a tree, a plant) aspect and the lovely eye color, and see if the name doesn't grow on you. If you read a lot of Southern fiction, such as Flannery O'Connor and Carson McCullers, you'll know Hazel is a well-used character name.

Heidi: As the title heroine of the 1880 classic, Heidi frolicked in the Swiss Alps, blond braids flying, thriving in the fresh mountain air and all that goat's milk. Since this is the crisp mental picture we all have of Heidi, those of you with roots in Algeria or Argentina may want to think it through a bit more before you saddle your olive-skinned, exotic darling with a name that practically yodels, it's so Swiss/German. But if you happen to be Swiss/German, the name is pure sunshine, and rarely heard anymore. Plus, it's a great way to honor a relative named Adelheide without actually naming the poor child Adelheide.

Helen: It may be a touch soon for a Helen-istic resurgence, as this name was quite popular as recently as the 1940s, but in about ten years or so, this ancient Greek beauty should regain some of its previous luster. A little Helen today might pine for such flash-in-the-pans as Hailey and Madison, but as she grows she'll come to appreciate the richness and depth of the name's most famous bearer, the mythical Helen of Troy. That fair lady possessed "a face that launched a thousand ships," a beauty so stunning she triggered the Trojan War. (Rent *Troy* for more inspiration.)

Henrietta: It's wildly outdated, eccentric, and patrician, but the right naming duo can invert those attributes, making it a quirky vintage find with a tie to royalty. Indeed, there have been a number of crowned ladies with this name, including Queen Henrietta Maria of England, the wife of King Charles I who patronized a famous troupe of actors in 1625, called Queen Henrietta's Men. Granted, it's more common in England (where Matilda and Eloise are in the top 100), but Henrietta is a good choice for bold parents stateside who have a taste for names as old as castles and knights. Choosing this name would also honor a Henry in the family. In the Nurse Matilda books by Christianna Brand, Henrietta was one of the exceedingly mischievous and innumerable Brown children.
Nicknames: Henny, Hettie, and Hattie

Hermione: Selecting this name will immediately identify you as a huge Harry Potter fan, in this day and age, when throngs of readers are camping in bookstore parking lots to get their hands on Harry and Hermione et al.'s latest tale. The name is a bit thick for these parts, but it has been lightened considerably by the book character and the appealing young actress Emma Watson, who portrays Hermione Jane Granger in the films. J. K. Rowling didn't make up the name by any means: Hermione was first a daughter of Helen in Greek mythology, and then the Queen of Sicilia in Shakespeare's comedy *A Winter's Tale*. Caution: Hermie falls flat as a nickname.

> J. K. Rowling didn't make up Hermione: She was first a daughter of Helen in Greek mythology, and then the Queen of Sicilia in Shakespeare's comedy *A Winter's Tale*.

Honoria: With Grace, Hope, and Faith playing hopscotch all over the place, you might consider this alternative. Honoria ("On-OR-ia") is a lovely, high-minded name, as old-fashioned as they come, and truly singular. Honoria was a character in Faulkner's "Babylon Rising."

Imogene: While this ultracool name would be a highly adventurous pick in these parts, the English wouldn't bat an eye. Over there, Imogene hovers in the mid- to late 40s on the baby-name popularity charts (where, on our charts, Kylie and Ashley hang out). You might want to knock off the final *e*, as offbeat songster Imogen Heap does, to help people pronounce it correctly ("IM-o-gen," not "Im-o-GENE"). In the Bard's play *Cymbeline*, Imogene was a sweet and charming princess, one of his most appealing female characters ever.

Nicknames: I.M., Imo, Mo

India: I highly doubt that anyone would want to name their baby girl after uptight India Wilkes from *Gone With the Wind*, but that's not to say that you can't use the lilting, sumptuous name anyway. Beautiful, silky-smooth India is richly exotic without being alien. Perhaps these attributes prompted glamorous and offbeat singer-songwriter Sarah McLachlan to choose India for her daughter. Like Jemima and Araminta, India has long been favored by the British upper crust. Indie is a little hipster of a nickname, too.

Nickname: Indie

Iris: This flower name in the bouquet zigs while the others zag. It's not for everyone, but that makes it a cool iconoclast. Iris sounds like the kind of girl who grows up to play bass in the hippest side-stage band. Jude Law and Sadie Frost (themselves particularly well-named) hailed their daughter Iris, which adds some cachet, not that the name needs any. In *The Tempest*, Iris appeared as one of three otherworldly messengers; she was represented by a rainbow.

> Iris is the flower name in the bouquet that zigs while the others zag.

Isabella: Though there have been a tidal wave of Isabellas in recent years (it's cemented in the top 5), I still can't help but view it as gloriously beautiful and somehow interesting, although there is now an Isabella in every classroom nationwide. It has a spectacular sound that rolls off the tongue in the most delightful manner. Okay, I'm gushing. To set your baby girl apart from the masses, go with Isabel, which is more restrained and quite a bit less used. You still get the fab Izzy and Belle in the package deal, although not the quaint Bella. Though it doesn't sound like a nun's name, Isabella indeed was a lady married to God in the Shakespearean "dramedy" *Measure for Measure*.

Nicknames: Bella, Belle, and Izzy

Isolde: Isolde was an Irish princess in Arthurian legend, the daughter of King Anguish even, so you know her saga was melodramatic. Indeed, she married a king, but later fell in love with Tristan, who rescued her from the evil clutches of various foes. This ravishing name is actually considerably more user-friendly than some of the Irish tongue twisters that we're hearing lately, such as Niamh ("Neev") and Saoirse ("Saresha"): Isolde is more or less pronounced phonetically—"Iz-OLD"—making it not only easy to say but vividly original. For more inspiration, be sure and rent *Tristan and Isolde* (2006) and check out Sophia Myles's portrayal of Isolde. Tristan is a top 100 name, so perhaps his great love Isolde will follow.

Nickname: Izzy

Trendy Names No One Knew Were Literary

Briana ❈ Chloe ❈ Jessica ❈ Jordan ❈ Olivia ❈ Vanessa

J

Jacinta: Jacinta is a gentle floral name (it's Spanish for "hyacinth") with the potential to cross cultural boundaries. Besides being very pretty and highly uncommon, it's an exotic twist on the current crop of trendy flower names. Jacinda Barrett is a beautiful Australian actress who has raised the profile of this name considerably. In "Legend of the Rose of the Alhambra" by Washington Irving, Jacinta is a tender and beautiful young girl who, being raised in a convent, came to flower "like an opening rose blooming beneath a brier."

Nickname: Cinta

Jane: This is one of those fundamentally solid, feminine names that still manages to charm and flirt. You can't go wrong with Jane. There is nothing plain about her; instead, she's a blessedly up-front and honest alternative to the fussy sugar puffs out there (not to name names). Adding to the appeal is the lit namesake: Miss Jane Austen, who's only one of the most revered and influential novelists of all time. Jane is also about twenty times less popular than Grace, which is reaching saturation.

> Looking for an alternative to top 20 Grace? Jane's not so plain anymore.

Jemima: Every baby name freak I know is in love with the name Jemima, bemoaning the fact that it remains a victim of imitation maple syrup. North Americans steer clear of this lovely, quaintly old-fashioned name because of the hyper-identification with you-know-who of pancake fame (but really, is Aunt Jemima such a bad affiliation?). In England, however, Jemima could hardly have a different image. There it's borne by such aristocratic beauties as Jemima Khan and is as stylish as India or Araminta, names we haven't yet cozied up to here. It would take a fearless baby namer to emancipate Jemima, but I think a few style makers will rise to the challenge in the near future. Jemimah was a character in Thackery's *Vanity Fair*, Ian Fleming's *Chitty Chitty Bang Bang*, and a delightful fowl was so dubbed in Beatrix Potter's "The Tale of Jemima Puddle-Duck."

Nicknames: Jem, Mimma

Jerusha: Whenever I come across this rare treasure, which means "inheritance," I am struck anew by its exotic loveliness and strength. A Bible name—Jerusha was a queen of Judah, the wife of King Uzziah, and the mother of the boy King Jotham—this tender moniker could be a grand option to overused biblical favorites such as Hannah, Abigail, and Sarah. In Jean Webster's *Daddy-Long-Legs*, Jerusha Abbott, an orphan whose name was selected off a headstone by the facility's headmistress, writes letters to a benefactor who

---

The Bard's Babes

Ariel ❊ Beatrice ❊ Celia ❊ Cordelia ❊ Imogene ❊ Iris
❊ Marina ❊ Octavia ❊ Ophelia ❊ Phoebe

---

pays her way through college so that she can develop her innate writing gifts. She is a delightful character—a kindred spirit to such literary beloveds as Josephine March and Anne Shirley.

Nicknames: Rusha, Ru

Jessica: After reigning for two decades as the most used girl's name, Jessica began to slowly decline in the nineties and as of 2006 had plummeted to number 73. What this tells us is that people have collectively decided the world is glutted with Jessicas, and it sadly has lost any vitality left over from the seventies and eighties. Don't get me wrong: I see the appeal. Jessica is a beautiful, sweet, and old-fashioned name with charm to spare. The nickname Jessie is fantastic, too. What will have to happen for Jessica to trump Emma is for a hundred years to pass, at which time someone will rediscover it and we'll start all over again. Jessica was, stunningly, a character in *The Merchant of Venice*.

Nicknames: Jess, Jessie

Jordan: Despite the fact that this sounds like the trendiest of inventions, Jordan has some interesting roots if you dig a little deeper. First, it's an exotic Middle Eastern country; it's also a river that plays no small part in the New Testament, foremost as the place where Jesus was baptized. It's also a long-standing surname, adopted, much like Morgan and Madison, for boys and then for girls. Unlike those two superstars, though, Jordan is still more popular for boys, which is a good thing if you want to nab this for your daughter. F. Scott Fitzgerald thought so when he gave his female character the name Jordan Baker in the ultimate American novel, *The Great Gatsby*. Jordana adds an extra flounce.

Josephine: Here's a delicious choice that could very well join the rise of two other oldies but goodies, Violet and Charlotte. With Josephine, you could honor a beloved Joe in your family tree, or pay tribute to Jo March of *Little Women* fame, one of the most cherished characters in fiction. If Josephine itself seems too long (although it's no lengthier than, say, Madeline), pluck a pleasing shorter form from a versatile selection. Feeny is an antique nickname, while the happy, hopeful Josie is near irresistible. Arbiter of vogue Vera Wang has a Josephine.

> With Josephine, you could pay tribute to Jo March of *Little Women* fame, one of the most cherished characters in fiction.

Nicknames: Jo, Josie, Feeny

Julia: The feminine version of Julius, Julia is a perennially stylish slam dunk. Classically beautiful yet not as overused as Emma, Sophia, or Olivia, this name is as polished as a silver tea set. This is an ancient appellation, too, dating back to biblical times (Julia appears in the Book of Romans) and Elizabethan England, where Julia figures in as a lady of Verona in *The Gentleman of Verona*. One sweet variation is the Dutch edition of Julia: **Julitta**, chosen by actress Marcia Gay Harden for her daughter. Julia was a character in George Orwell's *1984*.

Juliet: Through Romeo is a name that places way too much pressure on a guy, Juliet somehow sounds romantic without being ostentatious. Juliet Capulet is one of literature's most tragically romantic heroines, starring opposite her true love, Romeo, in Shakespeare's *Romeo and Juliet*. Their story didn't start with the Bard, though: in earlier versions Juliet was called **Giulietta**. In Verona, Italy, a bronze statue of Juliet stands in the courtyard of the house that reportedly had belonged to the real Capulets once upon a time. It's called Casa di Giulietta.

> Love Emma, Olivia, and Sophia? Classical sister Julia is much less used.

Juno: If you have a beloved June in the family, but find that grandma name a little lackluster, what about Juno? The month of June was named after Juno, the Roman queen of the gods, after all, so it wouldn't be a stretch to name Juno after June. At any rate, few girls' names end in *o*, which gives it a hip and bouncy groove. In literature, Juno appeared in Virgil's *The Aeneid* and also in Shakespeare's *The Tempest*.

K

Kalliope/Calliope: Name freaks were pleased when *Grey's Anatomy* introduced the character Calliope Iphigenia Torres O'Malley ("Callie"). It's a big fat Greek name for someone to live up to, and certainly not everyone's cup of retsina, but as Sara Ramirez's character shows, it can be done successfully, and by someone not of Greek heritage.

Calliope combines moxie with a poetic heart, which is fitting since, in Greek mythology, she was the muse of epic poetry, Homer's inspiration for *The Iliad* and *The Odyssey*. You can spell this with either a *C* or a *K*.

Nickname: Kallie, Callie

Katerina: A Russian spin on Katherine, Katerina is as gilded and luxe as a Fabergé egg. It sounds European yet not inaccessible to the North American ear. Fans of figure skating will think of the luminous Ekaterina Goordeeva—"Katya"—and indeed this gorgeously feminine name would be perfect for a future ice-skater or ballerina. Katya is adorable on a little girl, especially if you have Russian heritage in your background. In Dostoyevsky's *The Brothers Karamazov*, Katerina Ivanovna Verkhovtseva figures significantly.

In Dostoyevsky's *The Brothers Karamazov*, Katerina figures significantly.

Nickname: Katya

Katherine/Catherine: Ageless, regal, and gentle all at once, Katherine/Catherine has been one of history's best-loved names for good reason. If this formidable classic, a royal favorite for eons, appeals, please choose the wholly formed version. Yes, the full enchilada Katherine is quite highly ranked on popularity charts—about a hundred places above its nickname, Kate. But your child will love to have options with her name someday, if only in junior high, when she goes through the name-change phase. And this baby is loaded with options, from the breezy Kat/Cat to the stupendously well-liked Kate/Cate, to the ultraelegant Kay (Cay? Well, why not?). **Kit** is my favorite morph of all (see Kitty/Kit). The Bard, by the way, appointed one of his many royal princesses with Catherine in *Henry V*, and another character Katherine in his comedy *Love's Labours Lost*.

Nicknames: Kat/Cat, Kate/Cate, Katie/Catie, Kay, Kit, Kitty

Kitty/Kit: In this country, Kitty is something that's covered in fur whom you call to come in for a dish of Meow Mix. In England, though, Kitty is much more prevalent, and no one is phased in the least by its hyper-feminine wiles. Stateside I see it working only as an affectionate nickname for Katherine, as it appeared in *Pride and Prejudice* in the form of an occasional identification for one of the Bennett sisters. (Kitty was also the pet form of Ekaterina, Levin's love interest in *Anna Karenina*, as fans of that book know.) **Kit** is a different story, though—an extremely cute name with buoyant, pixilated charm. Sixteen-year-old Kit Tyler is the heroine at the heart of *The Witch of Blackbird Pond*, Elizabeth George Speare's Newbery Medal–winning 1959 novel.

L

Lara: When a friend of mine named her baby Lara, she was asked from time to time about being a *Doctor Zhivago* fan. She had no idea what people were talking about; all she knew was that Lara was sweet, compact, and more fascinating to her than Laura. This is Lara's appeal: it has four letters, is feminine, easy to spell, and, whether baby namers know it or not, still has some Russian allure via Boris Pasternak's 1957 novel of the Russian Revolution. Lara, the romantic female lead, was played by Julie Christie in the classic movie.

Laura: Laura has been the writer's muse since the days of Petrarch; he saw a woman with this name outside a church in Avignon in 1333 and was smitten to the core. Modern baby namers, though, are probably most inclined toward Laura because they spent many happy girlhood hours pouring over the *Little House* books by Laura Ingalls Wilder. Those now grown-up girls have a tender spot in their hearts for Wilder and the prairie pioneer stories she spun from her own childhood experiences. This is an especially pretty classic that won't make any waves but will always be a safe and gently stylish choice.

Lillian: This comeback kid was a smash hit during Victorian days and is an almost-smash hit today, some one hundred years later. It's the ultimate revival name, a serious yet sweet companion for Claire, Emma, Violet, Faith, and Amelia. Nickname Lily lightens things up, giving the name a two-for-one edge on its Victorian competitors. Lillian Reardon was the hard-nosed, superconfident, and ultra-glam female lead in Ayn Rand's novel *Atlas Shrugged*.
  Nickname: Lil, Lily

Lily: This flower name is so well-used that people don't heavily identify it as such anymore, like they do Daisy or Violet. As of 2006, Lily was the number 14 name on the popularity charts, and it could definitely go higher and become more crazy-popular (as in Emma-crazy). People just love Lily. It's delicate, yet with a certain strength and resonance. Like Emma, it's polished but also sounds darling on a little girl. If you like Lily but want something fresher, check out Lila or Layla, or even other blooms in the bouquet such as Violet or Daisy. Lily Bart was the doomed heroine in Edith Wharton's 1905 novel *The House of Mirth*.

Linnea: Looking for a flower name that hasn't been picked over? Linnea is a delicate, pink, bell-like wildflower named after the ecologist and botanist Carl Linneaus of Sweden. It was the perfect thing to call the little girl who learns all about Paris and lily ponds and impressions of light in the modern children's classic *Linnea in Monet's Garden* by Cristina Bjork and Lena Anderson. This is a very pretty, unusual name that suggests both art and books—how great is that? Linnea also carries a distinct impression of Scandinavia, although it's not limited to families with that background. A wildflower name with a lilting, European flair? You can't do much better than that.

> Linnea was the perfect thing to call the little girl who learns all about Paris and lily ponds and impressions of light in the modern children's classic *Linnea in Monet's Garden*

Lolita: This little tamale may be too hot to handle. Yes, it's a charming and cheerful name infused with vibrancy, verve, and sensuality, but is there too much of the latter to make this user-friendly for a little girl? It's hard to ignore Vladimir Nabokov's notorious novel *Lolita*, which all but turned the title character's name into an adjective describing sexually precocious young girls. The book was named by *TIME* magazine in 2007 as one of the top 10 most influential novels of all time, which means Lolita's hypersexual vibe is not going away, maybe ever. Lola is fabulous without the baggage.

Nickname: Lola

London: Gender-neutral London is strong and polished on a girl, and suggests someone who might grow up to have a passport with lots of stamps. Also, there's a female character on the popular tween show *The Suite Life of Zack and Cody* with this name, so there's a whole generation of kids who will be familiar with it. Literary references include Jack London's surname and Charles Dickens's habit of using his home city as a "character" in his novels.

Lorelei: This name, pronounced "Laura-lie," is a fascinating study in how television can affect what people are calling their babies. Right after Lauren Graham popularized her character Lorelei on *Gilmore Girls*, the name catapulted out of nowhere onto the charts. Although it's (very slowly) rising, this is still a highly novel and creative choice. Bonus: It's also one of the few beautiful German names (I'm German, so I can say that) that you can choose as an ethnic tribute name. In German folklore, Lorelei was the stunning siren with the glistening golden hair who lured untold boatfuls of men to their deaths on the Rhine River. Okay, so, she wasn't nice, but she did have a fabulous name! Classic movie buffs might recall Lorelei Lee as Marilyn Monroe's character in *Gentleman Prefer Blondes*, which was based on a novel written by Anita Loos (whom some have dubbed the originator of chick lit) in 1925.

Louisa: When one of our friends, a particularly skilled baby namer, dubbed her middle daughter with this jewel, I sighed happily. There is something so sweet and cozy about this name, yet it's as polished and smart as Louisa May Alcott, the author of the beloved *Little Women* series. The same ingredients that propelled Emma and Lily and Hannah to the top of the heap exist in full measure here. While this atypical choice sounds like an antique revival— which it is—the sporty shortie Lou saves it from being too Victorian. Louisa has all the makings of a hit, but I predict it will never even crack the top 100. The French spin, Louise, didn't sound too perky even a few years ago, but then Prince Edward and Sophie, the Countess of Wessex, revived it considerably by appointing their wee blue blood Lady Louise.

Nickname: Lou

Lucy/Lucetta/Luciana: It's hard not to fall in love with Lucy, one of the sweetest, friendliest names ever. Though it's ten times more popular in England (one chart shows it at number 8 over there), Lucy is gathering steam here, having cracked the top 100 for the first time in almost a century in 2006. This means the trail broken by Emma and Lily is being well trod on by Lucy. Lucy is the girl who reads *Little Women* up in her tree house before soccer practice. She's as well rounded as they come. Lucy has been affixed to all kinds of heroines in Dickens and Austen novels, and it also belongs to Lucy Pevensie, the littlest traveler through the wardrobe in the Chronicles of Narnia series. You can lengthen it into Lucinda or even Lucille (a slick pick for any fan of B. B. King) to add more versatility, but Lucy on its own simply sparkles. **Lucetta** and **Luciana** add a lush Italian flourish and an aura of old-world romance. Lucetta is Julia's maid in Shakespeare's *The Two Gentlemen of Verona*, and in *The Comedy of Errors*, Luciana is shocked to be pursued by her brother-in-law's twin, who she believes to be her sister's husband. Sounds like a problem.

Luna: Here's a luminous name rising slowly but steadily up the charts (but don't worry, it'll never be in the top 100): luminous Luna. This Italian and Spanish word for that milky white orb in the night sky has baby-name freaks over the moon, enchanted with its graces. Luna's tender, peaceful, and enchanting, quite the evocations from four little letters. In a world of sun worshippers, this moonlit name is perfect understated elegance. Luna was the goddess of the moon in Roman mythology.

Lydia: Lydia conjures images of a wellborn young lady wearing an Empire-waist gown, as Jane Austen's character in *Pride and Prejudice* did. Elegant without being affected, Lydia is a fine pick for a museum-going, arts-loving clan. (It even means "cultured one.") There's a biblical backbone here as well, as Lydia was a "seller of purple cloth" and a great supporter of the apostle Paul in the Book of Acts. Lydia has

Lydia is more playful than sister Austen names such as Catherine and Elizabeth.

intellect and reserve, yet is more playful than some Austen names. (Catherine and Elizabeth come to mind.)

Nickname: Lydie

Mabel: Anyone out there remember what Paul Reiser and Helen Hunt named their TV baby on *Mad About You*? Here's a clue (like you need one): it's an acronym for Mothers Always Bring Extra Love. Yes, it's saucy Mabel, which seems destined for refurbishment, even if a famous ninetie's TV baby didn't spark a wave of mothers bringing extra love to their baby's names. Why? It's got that trendy hard *a* sound, and it was a smash hit at the turn of the last century. These are the components that propelled Ava to the top. I admit, it's a mystery why this cheeky little lass hasn't caught on. If you like Violet and Ruby, do consider Mabel. It's simply adorable, neglected, and waiting for some really creative couple such as yourselves to restore it to its former glory. (By the way, Mabel is Shakespearean. Queen Mab was the wild and crazy queen of the faeries in *A Midsummer Night's Dream*.)

Nickname: Mab

Madeline: Like Emma, Madeline is a sweet, old-fashioned charmer that has shot up into the stratosphere of popularity in the last few years. Why? For starters, this should ring a few bells: "In an old house in Paris, that was covered with vines, lived twelve little girls in two straight lines...the smallest one was Madeline." Not only is Madeline the piquant little pixie beloved by readers of Ludwig Bemelmans's classic series, but from those very books came dolls, outfits, accoutrements—all associated with the name Madeline. Madeline's a dusty remnant from a gentler time, sister to Emma, Olivia, Sophia, and Isabella. And who can resist the nickname Maddy? Madeline offers much (though it doesn't lend originality). If that's your goal, check out Mirabella and Maeve, and if you just cannot let go of Maddy, Madeira is a lovely, fresh-sounding place name (an island in Portugal) that sounds spectacular on a little girl.

Nickname: Maddy

Margaret/Maggie/Maisie: Take another look at this staunch pillar and you may find it more appealing than you thought at first glance. Hardly any other female name has such fortitude, such a "don't mess with me" attitude; and yet, Margaret still seems ladylike and nurturing. Rare is the name with such an august history: Margaret's been born by queens, saints, and, most recently, Queen Elizabeth's sister, Princess Margaret. Margaret of Anjou was featured in Shakespeare's *Henry VI* (parts 1, 2, and 3) and *Richard III*. Plain (pear-free) Margaret appeared in *Much Ado About Nothing*. Margaret offers not only a strong, classic full form but oodles of nicknames and ethnic variations. Madge (Madonna's cheeky British nickname) has a great sense of humor, and Greta is darling. Smashing Maret is a Dutch/German spin. **Maggie** is a top 100 name on it's own (although I still recommend going with the full-fledged Margaret, and then calling your little girl whatever nickname you want). Maggie was a main character in Tennessee

Williams's play *Cat on a Hot Tin Roof*. **Maisie** is a sweet
and adorable old Scottish pet form of Margaret that sounds
very much in keeping with modern tastes. Besides the cute
Maisy Mouse series, Maisie also showed up in the Henry
James's 1897 novel *What Maisie Knew*.

Nicknames: Maggie, Maisie, Meg, Marge, Margie, Marg

Marianne: Marianne Dashwood was the "sensibility" to her
older sister Elinor's "sense" in Jane Austen's smash hit novel
Sense and Sensibility. No one who read the book (or, for that
matter, watched Kate Winslet's turn as Marianne) could
fail to feel tenderly toward this most tender of Austen's heroines, who always wore her heart on her sleeve. Going back
even farther, Maid Marian was Robin Hood's love as they
robbed from the rich and gave to the poor. These are both
superlative literary connotations, so it's a bit of a shame
that Marianne/Marian still seem tied to the fifties and sock
hops and poodle skirts. Still, Lillian is ascending, and Marian might well do the same thing.

Nickname: Mari

Marina: Just say the word out loud and you'll hear how
lovely it is. Marina is one of the prettiest names out there,
with wonderful evocations of sailboats, waves, and surf. In
Shakespeare's *Pericles*, Marina was born on a ship during
a storm at sea, hence her seaworthy name. Later, the vir-
ginal Marina is sold into slavery to a brothel; frustrated by
her stubborn virtue, the madam rents her out as a tutor for
respectable young ladies. (I know if I needed such a tutor,
a brothel is the first place I'd look.) If you love the sea or
you just like the gorgeous sound of Marina, it's quite rare,

hovering in the middle of the top 1,000. The variation **Marin** is an intriguing name on the rise, perhaps brought to public attention through the actress Marin Hinkle or a TV character played by Anne Heche in *Men in Trees*.

In Shakespeare's *Pericles*, Marina was born on a ship during a storm at sea, hence her seaworthy name.

Marlowe: Searching for something really peerless? As in, no peers will ever share this name with your child? Marlowe is a theatrical yet simply constructed name that wins points for a sound that rolls off the tongue, an "o" ending that pops, and a maverick vibe. Christopher "Kit" Marlowe was the English playwright who stormed the playhouses of London with such melodramas as *Tamburlaine*, preceding Shakespeare in writing blockbuster Elizabethan tragedies. Marlowe is *très chic*, but if you can't help yourself, you can call the girl Marly too. Irish actor Thorsten Kaye named his daughter Marlowe.

Nickname: Marly

Mary/Mamie: As of 2006, Mary is off the top 100 for the first time in about a millennium—literally. This is the bigwig girl's name of all time; the New Testament of the Bible mentions four Marys, including Mary, the mother of Jesus. Oodles of girls bore this Greek version of the Hebrew Miriam among early Christians, but then for several hundred years, the name was thought to be too holy to be worn by a mere mortal. Around the twelfth century, Christians started designating it once again for their daughters, and Mary reigned supreme as the number 1 girls' name for centuries. Linda booted Mary from her entrenched spot at the top in the late 1940s, and today Mary is conspicuously absent from playgrounds and preschools. Plenty of little Katharines, Sarahs, and Elizabeths are running around (these are all top 50 names), so at this point, believe it or not, choosing Mary would be kind of different. If you want a zippier version of the same basic Mary model, consider **Mamie,** a Mary pet form with more sass and old-timey quaintness. Mamie, rejiggered for her daughter Mary Willa by Meryl Streep, was a character in Henry James's *The Ambassadors.*

Matilda: What does someone as wildly ID'ed as Moon Unit Zappa name her child? Matilda Plum (those celebrities and their fruited names!), a choice that seems quite subdued altogether when compared to the mother's lunar moniker. But somehow, Moon's selection makes sense. Matilda is an old German classic, yet it also sounds sprightly (thanks to Roald Dahl's heroine) and quirky. The late Heath Ledger and Michelle Williams named their baby Matilda not long ago, which can only mean good things for this underused gem. For nicknames, you can circumvent trendy Madison and the overheated Madeline and still get Mattie via Matilda (and Tillie, too.) The movie *Nanny McPhee* was also based on the enchanting Nurse Matilda books.

Nicknames: Mattie, Tillie

Looking for an option to trendy Madison and over-heated Madeline? Opt for Matilda. You still get Mattie out of the deal.

Maud: It always pained me a little that my favorite author, *Anne of Green Gables* scribe Lucy Maud Montgomery, never used the cheeky, cute Lucy and instead went by Maud except on book covers. (Apparently Maude was a top 100 mainstay during the Victorian era, so she wouldn't have been alone by any stretch.) But recently I've been warming up to Maud, as it is cut from the same iconoclastic cloth as Olive, Harriet, Matilda, and Agatha, names that now sound quirky and sweet. Plus, Maudie is an adorable nickname.

Nickname: Maudie

Maxine: It's a stretch, but flapper girl Maxine could perk up, especially since Max is such a superstar for the boys. Because of this—and because we haven't heard it in several decades—Maxine has a better shot at rejuvenation than French sisters such as Nadine or Blanche. Also, don't discount the power of *X*, the hottest letter in the alphabet. Nicknames Max and Maxie are *très adorable*. Maxine was the vixen in Tennessee Williams's play *Night of the Iguana*.

Nicknames: Max, Maxie

May: Just three little letters, and what breezy, sunlit images spring forth from them! May is exceptionally graceful, pretty, and brimming with a fresh and life-affirming aura. If you like your names spare and unfussy, May could be a sparkling option along with sleek numbers such as Faith, Jane, and Ivy. Last popular around the 1890s to the 1920s, May is rarely heard these days and poised for new success. May Welland Archer was the perfect society wife in Edith Wharton's *The Age of Innocence*, and beloved author of *Little Women* Louisa May Alcott, claimed the designation for her middle name.

Maya: Maya is a warm, earthy name with a groovy global backbeat. Nowadays people of all ethnicities are using it (it's top 40), but Maya still retains some of its link to Central America and the Mayan culture. Luna, Freya, and Thea share those international qualities, but are much less trendy. Maya Angelou (born Marguerite Johnson) is an American poet, memoirist, and activist known for her autobiographical writings such as *I Know Why the Caged Bird Sings*. Her volume of poetry *Just Give Me a Cool Drink of Water 'Fore I Die* was nominated for the Pulitzer Prize.

Miranda: Of all his name concoctions, Miranda may be the Bard's finest. He wanted his characters' names to fit the essence of their personality, actions, and perhaps the challenges he would throw at them. Miranda he crafted from the Latin word *mirandus*, which means "admirable." In *The Tempest*, Miranda is so often admired by other characters for her tender heart and inner strength that they refer to her as "a wonder." This wondrous name has endured several centuries and is still used by parents drawn to its lyrical grace and loveliness. As Amanda slowly but surely slides out of the top 100, Miranda is always and forever a beautiful, still original, classic.

Uranus's small moon Miranda, discovered in 1948, was named after the Shakespearian character.

Miriam: Miriam has never really fallen out of fashion, nor has it ever been overused, which makes this a lovely selection for parents with a taste for the classics. In the Bible, Miriam fetched baby brother Moses out of the river in his basket. Her name is refined, sensitive, and intellectual. Short forms include the Star Trekish Miri and the homespun Mimi. Miriam was a character in *Sons and Lovers* by D. H. Lawrence.

> If You
> Like Maya,
> see Luna,
> Freya,
> and
> Thea.

Nicknames: Miri, Mimi

N

Nadia: If your family has jock genes, you might want to consider Nadia, which may be the all-time most athletic name of all, belonging to a sprinter, a tennis player, a skier, a triathlete, and of course a gymnast. Since Nadia Comaneci was the first to score a perfect 10, at the Montreal Olympics in 1976, her delicate, Eastern European name has ascended to the top 200. Like Katarina or Natalia, Nadia has that golden, Slavic beauty admired by so many. It's very feminine, yet with all the strength of an Olympic champion. In E. L. Konigsburg's Newbery Medal–winning novel *The View from Saturday*, Nadia Diamondstein is one of four sixth-graders who make their way to the New York State Academic Bowl.

Nadine: Around the 1920s and 1930s, French names were all the rage, including Nadine, which still retains some of its Francophone flavor eighty years later. Frenchified names have plummeted since the middle of the century and have yet to recover from sounding dated and a little bit boring, but Nadine hasn't been in style for such a long time that it's conceivable it will soon sound *nouvel* and novel again. Nadine Gordimer is a South African novelist and writer, winner of the 1991 Nobel Prize in literature and the 1974 Booker Prize for her novel *The Conservationist*.

Natasha/Natalia: Natalya (Natasha) Rosova is the principle female character in Tolstoy's *War and Peace*, which patient readers already know because they spent weeks (months?) with her when they read that imposing tome. Beguiling and lush Natasha came about as an affectionate nickname for Natalya, and though over the years it's lost some of its Slavic mystique, it's still an original choice that's not overused. Nattie and Tasha are both viable nicknames, should you desire such a thing. **Natalia** sounds fresher and more exotic today than nickname Natasha, not to mention romantic and alluring. Beware, though, that Natalia is creeping up the charts, bumping up against the top 100. Natalia was a character in Chekhov's *Three Sisters*.

Nicknames: Nattie, Tasha

Neeley: Readers of Betty Smith's classic *A Tree Grows in Brooklyn* know that Neeley is Francie's brother, but the name has real currency for a girl. It shares a common sound with Keely and isn't that far off from Nina. Some parents have already appropriated the traditionally male name Neal for their daughters, and Neeley makes it even more feminine. It's sporty and tomboyish, but it's feminine enough for Easter dresses and tea parties. A true find.

Nell: Once a nickname for Eleanor, this short but sweet charmer is due for at least a small-scale restoration. It's just as tidy as Jill or Jane or Anne, but much more unusual. Victorian, yet unfussy and intelligent, Nell is quaint without being flowery. In Dickens's *The Old Curiosity Shop*, Little Nell is a bright and beautiful little girl who lives with her grandfather in his shop of "curiosities." The famed establishment still stands in London, and someday you can take your own Little Nell to browse for some no doubt exceedingly curious items.

In Dickens's *The Old Curiosity Shop*, Little Nell is a bright and beautiful little girl who lives with her grandfather in his shop of "curiosities."

Niamh: Every day is St. Patrick's Day with this radiant Irish hit, ranked in the top 10 over there and heard on every block in County Sligo (and Clare, Galway, etc.). Here people usually have no idea how to pronounce it ("neev"), which proves to be a stumbling block. But if you are really, strenuously attached to your Irish heritage—even better if you have a genuine-article last name such as Flanagan or O'Malley—this lassie would make a daring statement. True, it would ensure a lifetime of spelling and respelling for your little Niamh, but heck, those who matter will get it right. In Celtic mythology, Niamh was a goddess who loved Oisin so much she gave him her horse, Embarr, who could run above the ground.

Nina: Nina would sound beautiful on a young Italian girl, a Russian ballerina, or a little Latina. It's simply global, and therefore makes a wonderful understated ethnic name for a variety of backgrounds. Nina has never gone out of style, but because it peaked at the turn of the twentieth century, it's also a Victorian revival name on top of everything else.

As you can see, Nina offers the whole package: grace, solidity, subtle ethnic overtones. Plus, it's eternally in vogue. Nina is the first name of British novelist Bawden, who wrote many popular juvenile books, including *Carrie's War*.

Nora has the kind of understated elegance Julia, Claire, and Ella have, but is much less used.

Nora: The Greeks scored over and over with fabulous names, and Nora is one of them, even though it sounds quintessentially Irish. (It has, in fact, had such long-standing popularity in Ireland that most people assume it is Irish.) Whatever Nora's provenance, it's beautiful, serene, and quietly on the rise, especially in affluent communities. Singer Norah Jones adds an *h*, which is fine but not necessary. This is the kind of understated elegance Julia, Claire, and Ella have, but Nora is much less used. Nora was the strong heroine of Ibsen's *A Doll's House*.

☆ O ☆

Octavia: This luxuriant, ravishing name rolls off the tongue gorgeously. Octavia was once used as the name for an eighth child, but now it sounds like one more O choice to add to Ophelia as an unconventional substitute for Olivia. Octavia has a musical ring to it because of its relationship to the word *octave*, which is also from the root word *octo*, for "eight." Octavia was, unfortunately for her, the wife of Antony, who loved Cleopatra in—what else?—*Antony and Cleopatra*.

Nicknames: Tavi, Tavia

Odessa: If you're looking for an alternative to Olivia yet don't feel quite ready for Ophelia, meet Odessa. Catherine the Great named her beautiful Ukrainian seaport city—a shining metropolis known for poets, opera singers, and pianists—after Homer's *Odyssey*. There are a few nickname options here: Odie and Dess are just two. This is definitely something to call a ballerina.

Nicknames: Odie, Dess

Olivia is freakishly popular, so why not think about more subtle, creative O options such as Odessa, Octavia, and Owen?

Olive: Back in its heyday, during Queen Victoria's reign, Olive was much more popular than flouncy cousin Olivia. Today, tastes have swung wildly in Olivia's direction, with that blockbuster sitting pretty in the top 10 and reserved relative Olive not having cracked the top 1,000 in seventy years. I actually prefer Olive. It's more subtle, and it has a certain quiet depth and richness that flashier Olivia can't touch. If you like the refinement and low-key sweetness that Violet, Pearl, and Fern offer, think about Olive. You still get the hip nickname Liv, by the way, but in a much less trendy package. Olive Higgins Prouty wrote *Now, Voyager* and *Stella Dallas*, both of which were made into glamorous films during Hollywood's Golden Age.

Nickname: Liv

Olivia: There are droves of Olivias all over the country, so freakishly popular is this name, which caught fire in the nineties and hasn't stopped to take a breath since. Despite its trendy vibe, the name is as antiqued as an early edition of *Twelfth Night*, where Olivia appears as a lovely countess whose fair hand is eventually won by Sebastian. (By all means arrange a marriage now, because Sebastian's on the rise too.) If you're looking for a ravishing and novel O name, this is not it (see Ophelia). Liv is a zippy little nickname, though. It's almost worth the price of being the next Jennifer.

Nickname: O, Liv

> Despite its trendy vibe, Olivia is as antiqued as an early edition of *Twelfth Night*, where Olivia appears as a lovely countess whose fair hand is eventually won by Sebastian.

Opal: Ruby's on the rise, and Pearl shows signs of perking up, but what about opalescent Opal? The national gemstone of Australia is also a name that shimmers with muted colors and soft lights. I could definitely see this dusty jewel being unearthed by artistic-minded parents who love its antique charm and its dash of old-lady quirkiness. Opal is known to readers as the winsome girl heroine of *Because of Winn Dixie*, and Opal Koboi is one of the main antagonists of the Artemis Fowl series.

Ophelia: This luxurious, wildly romantic name may not be as offbeat as you might think. In fact, Ophelia was not uncommon at all about a hundred years ago, which makes it ripe for consideration in our age of antique revivals. It's one of those sumptuous names that you just want to say out loud all the time—Mirabella and Francesca are two more—simply because they are so gorgeous. The beautiful Ophelia was Hamlet's love interest, a noblewoman from Denmark whose sad ending (she drowned herself) may have prevented her name from becoming too popular. But for those who are not intimately acquainted with Shakespeare, Ophelia sounds lush and lovely. (And besides, it would be a breath—a *gust*—of fresh air after a glut of Olivias.)

Orinthia: If the relatives become alarmed, try and calm them down with soothing references such as Cynthia and...well, that may be the only soothing reference, so keep it handy. Orinthia is an otherworldly name used by George Bernard Shaw in his 1929 play *The Apple Cart*. In the play's interlude, the character of King Magnus tells his mistress that her name is "full of magic," and he's right. The bewitching Orinthia also appears in an ancient English ballad entitled "The Pilgrim of Love." After choosing this for your little darling, you can certainly be assured that the ground is broken for Ulysses and Echo.

Owen: When singer Michelle Branch named her baby daughter Owen, she opened another name up for big cross-over potential. After all, on the girls' list, Jayden is a top 100 name, and Ryan is a top 500 name. Owen has the same breezy, soft sound that makes it a candidate for skipping over to the girls' side. Like Dylan or Spenser, a girl named Owen would be comfortable kicking soccer balls or kicking up her heels at a dance. Make sure you pair it with an incontrovertibly feminine middle name, such as Rose or Grace or Isabel, for a strikingly modern and superstylish package. Owen Glendower was the leader of the Welsh and Lady Mortimer's father in *Henry IV*, Part 1, by William Shakespeare.

Pamela: Everyone knows a Pam or two in her thirties or forties, which means her full name, honeyed and musical though it may be, isn't up for any kind of revival soon. Still, a little girl named Pamela would bring a new zing to the name—just don't call her the dated and yawn-worthy Pam. Ever. Though it sounds like someone your older sister graduated with, Pamela wasn't invented in the sixties. In fact, the name was concocted by Sir Philip Sidney for a character in his sixteenth-century poem "Arcadia."

Pandora: Whenever I come across this luxe name, it's always in some British novel and it always refers to an upper-crust, silver-spooned type of lady. Pandora is almost unheard of here, except for, of course, the bubbleheaded figure of Greek myths who opened a forbidden box and let loose wickedness into the world. (She did manage to close the box just in time to save Hope, humankind's only solace.) That's a bit of a heavy reference, but without it, Pandora shines with exotic beauty.

Paulina: This is an overlooked gem that has some winning attributes. First is the *a* ending that's so appealing to parents these days. In an era when we are glutted with Emmas and Isabellas, Paulina offers a sleek, old-fashioned charm with a throwback feel. Paulina is being used for Latinas, but it's also popular for all kinds of European ethnic backgrounds, such as that of Czech supermodel/author Paulina Porizkova and hockey player Wayne Gretzky's firstborn daughter. The wife of Antigonus, Paulina is a character in Shakespeare's *A Winter's Tale*.

Pearl: When a cast member (past or present) from SNL dubs a child something, pay attention. Between Will Ferrell's Magnus, Tina Fey's Alice, and Maya Rudolph's Pearl, these comics know how to pick a winner. Pearl is soft and shiny, still retaining almost all of its quaint, heirloom-ring-from-Grandma feeling, because it hasn't, unlike Ruby, caught on again. Pearl, like any gemstone name, shimmers a little more than the rest. Just one sleek syllable (unless you're Southern), Pearl makes a pretty middle name too. Pearl S. Buck (birth name Pearl Comfort Sydenstricker) was a missionary kid from China who wrote eloquently about the Chinese in her Pulitzer Prize–winning book *The Good Earth*. She was the first woman to win the Nobel Prize in Literature, in 1938. Pearl was also Hester Prynn's daughter in *The Scarlet Letter*.

Gemstone names such as Pearl, Garnet, Opal, and Ruby shimmer a little more than the rest.

Penelope: Odysseus and his wife, Penelope, were parted for twenty years in Homer's epic *Odyssey*. To him, she was as "longed for as the sun-warmed earth is longed for by the swimmer," the poem says. How swooning, how sigh-worthy! The ancient Greek name carries with it some of the same epic, romantic feeling, even though the Puritans gave it a bit of a starchy feeling for a couple hundred years. Penelope was the heroine of one of the great love stories of all time, not an uptight lady in a whalebone corset! Resurrect this glamorous name and you'll have people say to themselves, "Gee, why didn't I think of that one?" Why indeed. Bonus: Penny is a precocious, sweet nickname for a little tyke.

> Penelope was the heroine of one of the great love stories of all time.

Nickname: Pen, Penny

Phaedra: Phaedra has been written about, painted, and sung over for eons, such is the draw of her tragic love story from the myths. Though married, Phaedra fell in love with Hippolytus, and when it didn't work out—to say the least— well, you know what they say about hell having no fury like a woman scorned. Euripedes filled in more details with his 428 BC play, the ancient Greek tragedy *Hippolytus*, and many playwrights have continued to explore this intriguing character. But don't let Phaedra's errors of the heart divert you from her enigmatic and alluring name, which is more accessible than most of the mythological mouthfuls. Say it out loud a couple of times ("FAY-dra"). Isn't it lovely?

Nickname: Phay, Fay

Phoebe: This shimmering name is as ancient as the Bible (the Apostle Paul's friend, mentioned in Romans) and the Greek myths (Phoebe was a Titan, the daughter of Gaia and Uranus), but sounds really stylish for today's girls. Luminous Phoebe is a nature appellation (the Phoebe bird), a Shakespearean handle (Phebe appeared in *As You Like It*), and is the younger sister of Holden Caulfield in Salinger's *The Catcher in the Rye*. The meaning is fabulous, too: "bright, shining star." I could go on, but I don't want to gush too much for fear that half of you will pick Phoebe, propelling my baby girl's name into the upper echelons of the popularity chart. My husband liked it because of the bird, and I loved the biblical and literary references. For us, nothing could compare to the name we chose together for our own bright, shining star.

Phronsie: If you are willing to scale mountains and dredge the deepest rivers in search of a one-of-a-kind name for your singular sensation, take note of Phronsie. This quaint and quirky charmer is more unusual than even *Ph* sisters Phaedra and Philomena, but might be more functional than those names in the real world. In an era where nickname names such as Sophie and Josie are considered adorable, Phronsie actually might work as a more eccentric relative (like your cousin from Nova Scotia who is a mermaidologist). Phronsie was the baby of the Five Little Peppers, the one "at the center of everyone's heart." Her other Pepper sibs, created by Margaret Sidney in the late nineteenth century in her book *Five Little Peppers and How They Grew*, were Ben (Ebenezer), Polly (Mary), Joel, and Davie. Phronsie is a diminuative of Sophronia, if you really want to knock yourself out.

Pilar: A girl named Pilar cannot help but grow up to have an inbred sense of elegance and panache. It's hard to think of any choice that would so instantly impart chic and polish. A Spanish name, derived from the "pillar of the church," Pilar has a fortitude other names can only dream about. Pilar Gitano was a Gypsy and a pivotal character in Ernest Hemingway's *For Whom the Bell Tolls*. The best part may be that it is extremely unusual, and your Pilar is sure to be singular among her friends and classmates.

Pippi: Red-haired, gap-toothed, freckle-faced Pippi will always be all those things because of Pippi Longstocking, the fearless, fun-loving girl who engages in adventures with her roommates, a monkey, and a horse. As in every child's fantasy, her parents are nowhere to be found, and Pippi (with a level of autonomy that freaked out critics of Astrid Lindgren's inaugural Pippi book in 1945) is a free spirit to the extreme. But how shackled can you be when your full name is Pippilotta Delicatessa Windowshade Mackrelmint Efraim's Daughter Longstocking? If Pippilotta is too unshackled for you, think about Pippa, an effervescent contraction of the British fave Phillippa.

Victorian Valentines

Belle ❊ Charlotte ❊ Delia ❊ Fern ❊ Flora ❊ Lily
❊ Louisa ❊ Nell ❊ Phoebe ❊ Ruby

Pollyanna/Polly: I'm a glass-half-full gal myself, but I'm still glad I don't have a be-cheerful-or-else name such as Pollyanna, the queen of all optimistic names. (It makes even Hope and Joy seem a little down.) Since the publication in 1913 of Eleanor H. Porter's best-selling novel *Pollyanna*, the name itself entered the language (*Pollyannaism*, a noun, and *Pollyannaish*, an adjective) to describe someone who's so cheerful, she's almost in la la land. Stick with this as a sunshiny middle name or whack off *anna* altogether and go with the still-peppy **Polly**. Polly could be a real contender as parents look for something in that stylistic sweet spot of recognizable but uncommon, unexpected but likeable, and just a heartbeat away from past biggie Molly. Polly was also one of the *Five Little Peppers and How They Grew* kids.

Pomona: Gwyneth could have just called the child Pomona (which means "apple") and caused a lot less ruckus. In Roman mythology, Pomona was the goddess of fruit trees, gardens, and orchards. In nineteenth-century statues and building decorations she is usually shown carrying either a large platter of fruit or a cornucopia.

Portia: Here is a vibrantly Shakespearean name that evokes the Globe Theatre and Elizabethan players and all things related to the Bard. Portia is a glamorous and exotic creature, brought down to earth somewhat by actress Portia de Rossi. One issue with the name is that it sounds exactly like the luxury sports car, spelled Porsche, but that shouldn't keep you from choosing this rare beauty. Portia is best known as the dazzling lawyer (disguised as a man) in *Merchant of Venice*, but a Portia appeared as well in *Julius*

Caesar. There was also an African American character with this name in Carson McCullers's *The Heart Is a Lonely Hunter*.

Quimby: Kirby, Bailey, Kennedy…Quimby. Okay, so it's a stretch, but work with me a minute before tossing the idea out of hand. Surnames are white hot, especially Irish ones, and close cousin Quincy is already making inroads for girls; Quinn is already well established. Paired with a sweet, feminine middle name—Rose, Grace, Jane—Quimby could work as a highly stylized and quirky/adorable girls' name in the right family (maybe Diane Keaton's, who has a daughter named Dexter?). Plus, you get the phenomenally cute abbreviation Q, which is a big selling point. Quimby is the most apt last name of the fabulous Ramona the Brave of the beloved Beverly Cleary books.
Nickname: Q

Quintana: When I first read about Quintana Roo, the daughter of literary icons Joan Didion and John Gregory Donne, I was over the moon for this spectacular name. It's not often that a name pops out of the ordinary and simply crackles with vibrancy and unusual beauty. Quintana is a place in both Mexico and Brazil, and means "the fifth daughter." Quintana's Latin sizzle is brought down to earth by its quirkiness. **Quin** is an endearing short form.
Nickname: Quin

R

Raleigh: There's a market for Haleigh, Kaleigh, Riley, Kylie, and Braleigh, so there could be takers for Raleigh, a name that incorporates all the trendiest sounds of the day with a sturdier Renaissance underpinning. It is also the name of a city in North Carolina, and can be used along the lines of Savannah and Brooklyn. Sir Walter Raleigh was one of the foremost poets of the Elizabethan Age. As an explorer, he was also responsible for establishing the first English colony in the New World at Roanoke Island in present-day North Carolina.

Ramona: Okay, your child will suffer for ten minutes when some oaf in second grade calls her "Ramona the Pest," pointing to the much-loved youth novel by Beverly Cleary. How come no one ever remembers *Ramona the Brave* or *Ramona Forever*? Cleary wrote a stack of books about the cute, impish Ramona Quimby, rendering her a fondly remembered fictional heroine of childhood. Because of her, this name is instantly sassy, wide-eyed, and a tad eccentric around the edges, much like actress Maggie Gyllenhaal, who gave this peach of a name to her baby daughter.

Nickname: Mona

Rebecca: One of the purest and most dignified of the classics, Rebecca dates back thousands of years to the Old Testament (where it was spelled Rebekah). It's doubtful that modern parents would want to shorten this, certainly not to Miss Class of '87 Becky, but they may trim it here and there to Becca or Beck. Certainly, the full name will have the most appeal, as a sweet yet sturdy model of feminine beauty. Be aware that Rebecca is still a top 100 name, and probably always will be. *Rebecca* was a 1938 novel by Daphne du Maurier, the heroine of *Rebecca of Sunnybrook Farm*, and a beautiful and noble character in Sir Walter Scott's *Ivanhoe*.

Nickname: Becca, Beck

Regan: I met a Regan once (spelled Raegan) who said her mother, an English major, was in labor and couldn't remember if Regan was the good daughter or the bad daughter in *King Lear*. (Cordelia was the virtuous one, FYI.) So she got the wicked daughter's name, and all in all it worked out spectacularly well. The breezy, tomboy personality of her name suited her far better than lacy Cordelia. And that's the discussion of this name in a nutshell. You certainly wouldn't want your baby girl to emulate Princess Regan's ways, but it may suit your tastes perfectly anyway. It's presidential, too, which may be positive or not, depending on your bent.

Romola: Up-and-coming British actress Romola Garai brings a vibrant new identity to this satisfyingly rich and weighty Italian name. The pronunciation is "ROM-ulla," not "Rom-OLA," which may cause some confusion over the course of someone's lifetime (though not more than most creative names). *Romola* was an 1863 novel set in Renaissance Florence by George Eliot, aka Mary Ann Evans.

Rosalind: Here's a Shakespearean name that sounds distinctively Shakespearean (unlike, say, Jessica). With great abbreviation options such as Rose and Rosa or even possibly Lind or Sal (okay, I'm joking about the last one), Rosalind is romantic and offers nice versatility. In *As You Like It*, Rosalind was the woman Orlando was so besotted with he couldn't help himself from posting little love poems about her on trees. They are one of the Bard's most dreamy couples. "All the world's a stage," the playwright opined in his famous monologue in this comedy. A girl with a theatrical name such as Rosalind should fit right in.

> Rosalind and Orlando are one of the Bard's dreamiest couples.

Nicknames: Rose, Rosa

Rose: Tons of folks have used the richly evocative Rose as a middle name, and why not? It beats the pants off Lynn and Sue. Rose has also been quite well-used as a first name, especially during Victorian days when it was a top 20 smash. Parents who are drawn to the one-syllable simplicity and old-fangled charm of Grace, Hope, and Faith might take a peak at sweet Rose. It's reserved and modest, yet also can yield the more outgoing and fun Rosie. More flower names in the bouquet include Iris, Lily, Violet, and Daisy. Johnny Depp went turbo-floral with his selection of Lily Rose. Rose Wilder Lane was the only surviving child of Laura Ingalls Wilder and Almanzo Wilder. She is most famous for collaborating—to what extent is unknown—with her mother on the beloved Little House on the Prairie series.

Nickname: Rosie

Ruby: Lily, Sophie, Ruby...all the old belles of the ball are back for another dance. Parents love the blend of quaintness and vitality these Victorian revivals offer, and Ruby may be the shiniest resurgence of all. Even compared to other semiprecious stones such as Pearl and Opal, Ruby is the most sparkling gem in the jewel box. So much do I admire this turn-of-the-century beauty I would bestow it on another daughter—if we had one, which we don't. Tobey Maguire just named his firstborn Ruby, though, which means this gorgeous name is on the radar in a new way. In *Anne of Green Gables*, Ruby Gillis was one of Anne's school chums.

A_{va,} Sophia, and Lily's dance cards are full—why not waltz around with Ruby, a sister belle of the ball?

Rumer: Bruce Willis and Demi Moore's firstborn Rumer is grown, and somehow her name has never really caught on like so many celebrity baby handles do. Maybe it's because Rumer is so close to our word for tittle-tattle. Still, this is a sleek and serene name. Rumer Willis's parents were inspired by Margaret Rumer Godden, who wrote sixty books under the name Rumer Godden, including the best known, *The Greengage Summer*, which was made into a film. Godden, an Englishwoman, was born and raised in India and returned there as an adult to start a dance school for girls.

Ruth: A hundred years ago, Ruth was ranked fifth on the girls' baby-name chart. How times have changed. Now this gentle, soft-spoken biblical classic is sorely neglected while Rylee has her day in the trendy sun. Ruth is a virtue name, with connotations of mercy and friendship; there's also an outstanding biblical role model to consider, Ruth the wife of Boaz and the ancestor of David and Jesus. There's no nickname, and some of you like that, but for others, Ruthie is as cute as Gracie, and much less used. I think it's time for a Ruth revival. Grace reigns supreme right now, but those on a quest for a one-syllable classic with virtue need look no further. In E. M. Forster's *Howard's End*, Ruth Wilcox is the tradition-bound matriarch of the book title's Edwardian estate.

Sarah: Sarah will never go out of style, which is part of the appeal that has lured countless parents since Bible times. The name means "princess," although it really doesn't have that kind of pampered image. Because of its durability, this timeless tag is more in line with Patricia MacLachlan's *Sarah, Plain and Tall*. Sarah is pretty, soft, strong—the trifecta of what most people look for in names. The good news is this isn't a trendy name, but the bad news for some baby namers is that Sarah is somewhat overused. If originality is not your aim, and you love Sarah as so many others have, why not add a flourish with a Kate or Jane or Rose? Sadie is an old nickname of Sarah, too, which adds flexibility. Sarah Orne Jewett was the Maine novelist who wrote "The Country of the Pointed Firs."

Nickname: Sadie

Sawyer: Like Spencer and Owen, Sawyer gets a make-over on a girl. It's got sass, style, and a lot of backbone, as all boys'-names-for-girls have. Wouldn't Mark Twain be amazed to find out that parents of 2008 and beyond are naming their daughters after his freckle-faced hero? He'd probably be pleased. Sawyer is a spunky, fashion-forward name, not even on the top 1,000 for girls—yet.

Scarlett: If you're thinking you might have a Little Miss Sassy Pants on the way, Scarlett might be the perfect name for her. In addition to being linked to the eternal spitfire Scarlett O Hara of *Gone With the Wind* fame, this name has a new face: luminous blonde actress Scarlett Johansson, whose ultravibrant appellation has shot up in a direct trajectory with her fame. Scarlett's bolder than Savannah, and more creative than Sierra. It's a true spark plug.

> Scarlett's bolder than Savannah, and more creative than Sierra.

Scout: Again, we must tip our hats to the Demi Moore/ Bruce Willis baby-naming conglomerate. They had the big guts to use Scout as a name for their second daughter, and conventional wisdom has changed ever so slightly since. Of course, there hasn't been a rash of Scouts per se, but people are now much more accustomed to this as a given name as opposed to a pet name. Scout is definitely one of the most tomboyish names out there, and it might be kind of a mismatch on a frilly girlie girl. But then again, the beloved character Scout (aka Jean Louise Finch) in *To Kill a Mockingbird* was a cute, scrappy little thing who wins hearts every time someone reads about her pluck and goodness. Thanks mostly to her, Scout is useable in the real world, especially as a middle name.

Seneca: When you think of Anika, Danika, and even Vivica, Seneca seems more approachable. It's robust, unyielding—there's nothing namby pamby about Seneca. Indeed, the meaning of Seneca as an Iroquois nation is "people of the standing rock." If these are qualities you'd like to cultivate in your daughter, this is a bold and out-of-the-ordinary choice. Seneca was a Roman dramatist whose tragedies, including *Phaedra*, shaped the work of such luminaries as Shakespeare.

Shiloh: The Jolie-Pitt Naming Multinational launched this stupendous Hebrew place name into baby name orbit. In the Bible, Shiloh was the focal point of Israel's worship, a holy place in the Promised Land. In history, it was a Civil War battle site. Now, it's a beautiful baby girl, with a strong, determined, and adventurous name that other parents are sure to jump on. *Shiloh* (yes, I know he was a beagle) is Phyllis Reynolds Naylor's 1992 Newbery Medal–winning novel.

Nickname: Shi

Sojourner: Line up, seekers of justice, for one of the most declarative, unshackled, freedom-loving names ever given. Sojourner Truth (née Isabella Baumfree; she changed her name in 1843) was born a slave and

Line up, seekers of justice, for one of the most declarative, unshackled, freedom-loving names ever given: Sojourner Truth.

grew up to become a famous abolitionist. Her best-known speech is "Ain't I a Woman?," and her memoir, *The Narrative of Sojourner Truth: A Northern Slave*, was published in 1850. It's one of a kind, just like the grand lady who gave herself that name.

Somerset: If Summer is too seasonal and Sonnet too bluntly poetic, you may want to consider Somerset. It certainly is a lovely-sounding word that rolls off the tongue, but then again, it's also probably too fanciful for most. I have heard it in the real world, and I must say it still seems ostentatious. If you love Somerset anyway, think about the middle name slot, the perfect spot for something whimsical and precious. W. Somerset Maugham was the English playwright, short-story writer, and novelist best known for the incredibly depressing *Of Human Bondage*.
    Nickname: Somer

Sonnet: We all like to wax poetic about our children, so why not refer to them as living poems? Okay, so this might be a little over the top for some, but Sonnet has a pretty sound and the meaning is richly evocative. It's slightly hippie-ish, yet this side of outlandish, which means it would work extremely well as a middle name. A girl with the first name Sonnet (actor Forest Whitaker used this for his daughter) may enjoy her poetic name until she struggles with iambic pentameter in English class.

Sophie/Sofía: I always vowed never to choose a name for one of my kids that would ever appear on the top 100 (although that is hard to predict), but I came awfully close with Sophie, such was my admiration for the name. Sophie is adorable and quaint, and it still has a vestige of Old World charm. (It's both the French and the German form of Sophia.) It sounds like it could belong to a balle-rina—or a softball pitcher. Sophie, which belonged to a Miss Wackles in Dickens's *The Old Curiosity Shop*, could induce other parents to break their top 100 rule, too. (Okay, so I still pine for it!) Sophia, meanwhile, is completely out of control, reaching number 7 in the baby-name rankings. That final *a* ending adds some sophistication and Latin flair. Sofía is a more exotic spelling, and was borne by Sofía de la Piedad in Gabriel García Márquez's *One Hundred Years of Solitude*.

Spenser: People who can't stand girls' names for boys are cringing right now, while others are perking right up. Just like Riley, Bailey, and Taylor, Spenser could easily cross over from the boys' list. It's supercute on a little girl, even though most people will think of it as a boy's name—talk to Ryann and Kevyn's parents about that. Edmund Spenser wrote *The Faerie Queene*.

Stella: Stella sounds like a flapper girl with cheeky charm and a sassy sense of humor. Now that enough time has elapsed since the last time Stella was in vogue (in the 1930s it started to dip downward), we can view it with fresh eyes as a spitfire, life-of-the-party name. It's on the rise, sure to bump into old gal pals

> Now that enough time has elapsed since the last time Stella was in vogue, we can view it with fresh eyes as a spitfire, life-of-the-party name.

Ruby and Lucy in the near future. In Tennessee Williams's play *A Streetcar Named Desire*, Stella Kowalski is Blanche DuBois's sister.

Sula: Folks, gather round for a name so distinctive and unusual it does not appear in most, if any, baby-name books. Ta da! Here it is, because Sula Peace is the title character of Toni Morrison's 1973 novel *Sula*. This character is rebellious, complicated, and mostly maddening, though in the end she actually unifies the black community of Bottom where she lived out her days. She rebelled against every social custom, yet had a fulfilling life despite her wicked acts—and there's something to be said for that, Morrison implies. Even though the name has a striking African beat, it's Icelandic, and means "the sun." I think it's sumptuous, exotic, and yours for the taking.

Sula, the title character of Toni Morrison's 1973 novel, doesn't appear in most, if any, baby-name books.

Nickname: Su

Sylvia: Unlike sugar puffs such as Kaylee and Brandi, pretty-sounding Sylvia has a solid feel to it. But I can't help but think Sylvia is in Boca, playing canasta and wearing a muumuu. Maybe that's just me, because I *have* heard it recently as a twin name (paired with Nash) in an artsy family. At any rate, Sylvia Plath was an American poet, novelist, short-story writer, and essayist best known for *The Bell Jar*, her semiautobiographical novel.

Nickname: Sylvie

T

Tabitha: Can we get past the cat thing for five seconds and focus on this name's most excellent qualities? Playful and lovely, Tabitha enchants with roots as old as ancient Greece and as new as that cute little nose-twitching kid on *Bewitched* (a role that lends a bit of supernatural fairy dust). In the Bible, Tabitha was a disciple of the early church and known for her kindness; she was raised from the dead by Peter in the Book of Acts. This is such a sparkling, sweet name, it's a wonder it isn't overused. In books: Okay, so Tabitha Twitchett was Tom Kitten's mother in the Beatrix Potter story. Let's look beyond the feline associations (sure to be harmless, indeed!), because this name is worth it. Tabitha-Ruth ("Turtle") Wexler was a character in *The Westing Game*, the 1979 Newbery Medal winner by Ellen Raskin.

Nicknames: Tab, Tabby

Tallulah: This is one of those luscious, say-aloud names that just roll off the tongue. A Native American name, Tallulah has somehow made its way to Europe, where vogue folks such as Simon Le Bon have picked it for their girls. Tallulah was also chosen by American glitterati such as Bruce Willis and Demi Moore (them again!), and Patrick Dempsey. I predict this dynamic choice will catch on, especially when people realize you can get the adorable nickname Lulu out of it. Tallulah is a name in the Maisie Mouse children's book series.

Nickname: Lulu

Tamsin: Tamsin is one of those mysterious creatures that somehow manages to be accessible, too, like some treasure found in a bazaar in Morocco that looks perfect on your living room wall. It is definitely of the hard-to-match, hard-to-peg milieu, like Aniya, Greer, Tatum, Shiloh, or maybe even Apple. It's gorgeous, glamorous, superfresh, and hardly ever heard on this side of the ocean, though it does get some play in England. Don't use the nickname Tammy, though, or I will have to find you and administer a stern tongue-lashing. Tamsin appears in *A Few Green Leaves* by the British novelist Barbara Pym.

Nickname: Tam

Tennyson: Oh, so you think this is a boy's name and I've finally flipped my lid? Not so fast there, dear reader. Tennyson belongs to at least one woman, a friend of mine whose parents admired the poet Alfred, Lord Tennyson. The guy who uttered such immortal bon mots as "better to have loved and lost" was one of England's most revered poets. As a girl's first name, this is like a luscious Austin Cooper, all souped up and detailed: it's got rhythm and flow (appropriately enough), striking good looks, and an aural beauty that could inspire any number of admirers to scrawl out a rhyming couplet or two. If someone objects—"What are you going to call her, Tennis?"—say you will call her Tennyson,

In Bloom

Clover ❋ Daisy ❋ Fern ❋ Flora ❋ Hazel ❋ Iris
❋ Jacinta ❋ Lily ❋ Rose ❋ Violet

and then murmur, "Theirs not to reason why,/Theirs but to do and die." That'll clam 'em up. (My friend often goes by "Tenny," if you must produce a short form.)

Nickname: Tenny

Tess: If you like the compact, antique style of one-syllable hits such as Grace, Kate, and Claire, do check out Tess, a pretty miniature of Theresa. It has all the femininity and fortitude of those top 100 gals, but without the overuse. Tess stands strong without any adornment, but if you want to modernize it a bit, you could add an *a* at the end for Tessa. *Tess of the d'Urbervilles: A Pure Woman Faithfully Presented* (1891) is considered Thomas Hardy's ultimate work.

> If you like the compact, antique style of one-syllable hits such as Grace, Kate, and Claire, do check out Tess.

Thea: Thea would be a stylish surprise and a novel pick as well. Originally a pet form of Dorothea, this name presents an image of intuitiveness and tranquility. Refined yet not staid, Thea sounds like a girl who paints and dreams and has a pet duck named Araminta. It's quiet creativity at its best. Thea Kronberg was Willa Cather's heroine in *Song of the Lark*, an artist who leaves her hometown to go to the big city to fulfill her dream of becoming a famous opera star.

Thomasin/Thomasina: Georgia and Charlotte both sound completely sweet and accessible, so why not go out on that feminization limb and choose Thomasin or Thomasina? In the right family, this could be a major fashion statement, a museum-quality name that packs a stylish surprise. Like Phillipa, this name has had more use in England, but it's rare even there. Thomasina is so pretty and romantic, without being a bit fussy. Thomasin was a winsome young girl in Thomas Hardy's *Return of the Native*. The novelist introduced her with these words: "Mrs Yeobright saw a little figure... undefended except by the power of her own hope." Tommy is adorable as a nickname, and a Tommy Girl even has her own perfume.

Nickname: Tommy

Toby: If you're attracted to boys' names for girls, Toby is quite a find. Like Dylan, Morgan, Reece, et al., Toby started out on the masculine side, as a nickname for Tobias, but the history of the name dates back thousands of years, at least to the ancient Greeks. It's buoyant and sweet on a little girl, and novel on a grown woman. The best part is, very few parents are appropriating this one for the girls, so you could really be a vanguard here.

Sir Toby Belch was a character in *Twelfth Night* who was witty and full of puns. Those are his only positive attributes so don't look for an inspirational role model here. Maybe you'll have better luck with Uncle Toby, a character in Sterne's *The Life and Opinions of Tristram Shandy, Gent*.

Tristan: Because Tristan rhymes with Kristen, and it's *this-close* to Trista, it has some serious currency for the girls. As a boy's name, Tristan is sensitive and poetic, but on a girl, those attributes come with backbone and tomboy-ish charm. Tristan's a top 100 name for boys, but with its soft sound it could easily catch on for the girls too. Tristan was one of the Knights of the Round Table and also the legendary lover of Isolde.

Nicknames: Tris, Trist

Trixie: A nickname for Beatrix, Beatrice, or Patricia (a stretch, but there it is), Trixie brims with sass and bright-eyed energy. That *x* in the middle generates all kinds of spunk and personality. Trixie Belden, girl detective, lived at Crabapple farm and helped perpetually baffled authorities solve mysteries with her best pal, Honey. The well-loved series, launched in 1948, eventually spawned thirty-nine books, went out of print for years (the abomination!), and is now back where it belongs: in the hands of preteen girls reading under the covers with flashlights.

Nickname: Trix

Una: A true iconoclast, Una may appeal to parents in search of something really different but not complicated. Thanks to Uma Thurman, people are semiversed in the idea of a three-letter *U* name. For those who dig it, Una has a spectacular literary heroine in Spenser's personification of the unity of the church, and truth

> Una has a spectacular literary heroine in Spenser's personification of the unity of the church, and truth itself.

itself. In *The Faerie Queene*, Una has wild adventures involving knights and castles and dragons. **Oona** O'Neill was Eugene O' Neill's daughter and Charlie Chaplin's wife.

Ursula: I doubt the masses will ever overindulge in this Slavic-sounding name meaning "a female bear." But those of you on a quest for a *U* name (it could happen), or wondering about the feasibility in this day and age of honoring your great-grandmother Ursula, take heart. First of all, the letter *U* is almost unheard of as a starting vowel, so you would be safely iconoclastic there. Also, I've heard this rather ursine name trimmed to Ursi and Uschie, which are cute, quirky, and cublike. Ursula was a waiting gentlewoman attendant on Hero in *Much Ado About Nothing*.
  Nicknames: Ursi, Uschie

Valeria: A frilly, superfeminine name that just might catch on even more than it already has, Valeria ("Valerie-a") is the Spanish form of Valerie. Though Valerie is too young for any kind of name revival (it peaked in the sixties) and too old to sound fresh for today's baby namers, Valeria is a different story. Infused with some Latinate salsa, global worldliness, and a dash of sensuality, this baby's climbing up in the charts, especially within the Hispanic community. In Shakespeare's *Coriolanus*, Valeria was a lady of Rome.

Vanessa: Vanessa was one of the Cosby kids, which sounds about right considering the name's raging popularity in the

1980s. Oddly enough, though, this ultragirlie name has an august literary history dating back to 1713, when Jonathan Swift took a piece of his lover's last name, Vanhomrigh, and added her pet name, Esse (for Esther), for the resulting Vanessa. His autobiographical poem "Cadenus and Vanessa" minted the name. Vanessa is still quite trendy, especially among African American families. *Vanessa* was also a 1933 novel by British novelist Hugh Walpole.

Velvet: First of all, the horse was named Pie and the girl was named Velvet, just to clear up any confusion. I'm talking about *National Velvet*, the 1935 book by Enid Bagnold, which was made into a smash hit movie in 1944, starring twelve-year-old Elizabeth Taylor as Velvet. The plucky young Velvet saves her horse from the knacker's yard and, disguised as a boy and aided by her father's hired hand, trains it for the Grand National steeplechase. I can see the possibilities here for a very horsey family, but otherwise it might be a tad too fabric-related for functionality as a name.

Verena: Extremely rare and unusual sounding, Verena has a pleasing feminine lilt with a robust core (the meaning, from the same root word as *verity*, is "integrity"). This European-esque name would definitely give you the originality you crave, if in fact you crave such a thing. Verena was the rather fractious aunt to an orphaned boy in *The Grass Harp* by Truman Capote and appeared as the pretty, budding feminist in *The Bostonians* by Henry James.

Verlaine: This is a French-infused singular choice that also yields the cute nickname Lanie. Paul-Marie Verlaine, who died in 1896, is considered one of the greatest French poets of the fin de siècle period, which means the latter half of the nineteenth century.

Nickname: Lanie

Viola: With all the buzz attending Violet these days, classical sister Viola is waiting quietly in the wings. An overtly musical name (parents who know their way around a treble clef are choosing Aria and Adagio these days), Viola is gentle, serene, and rich. In her heyday at the turn of the century, Viola was hotter than Violet, a top 60 name for three decades. Shakespeare's Viola is one of his most distinctive and well-known characters. In *Twelfth Night*, the twin sister of Sebastian is shipwrecked, and then spends the rest of the play disguised as Cesario, a man, which causes problems because she is in love with Orsino, also a man.

Nickname: Vi

Violet: Violet has three images: She's having raspberry cordial in the parlor with her best friend, Opal; she's a gap-toothed cutie with grins that could melt a heart of stone; and third, she is the droll teen superhero from *The Incredibles*. In short, Violet is the ultimate Victorian revival, a modern girl with an old-fashioned soul. One hundred years ago, our gal Vi was sporting huge puffed sleeves and taking elocution courses. Today she's being born by such high-profile dolls as Violet Affleck (daughter of Ben and Jennifer Garner), and the name seems destined for bigger popularity (although I predict it will never reach

If you like Violet, see Viola.

Lily status; it's *too* old-fashioned for most). I love this name to pieces, and apparently others share the sentiment. Violet was a rather spoiled, bratty character in *Charlie and the Chocolate Factory* by Roald Dahl.

Violet's having raspberry cordial in the parlor with her best friend, Opal.

Nickname: Vi

Virginia: If Georgia continues to rise, there's no doubt Virginia will follow. This is a heartily American name with deep roots as old as the United States. It's also been ninety years since the name was in the top 10, making it ripe for renewal. There's no need to caution you about the word *virgin*, because that's probably your chief objection anyway. But if you like Virginia's grand femininity and historical strength, you can always call her Ginny or even Ginia. Virgie might be out of the question for the indefinite future as it seems mighty close to *virgin*. Virginia Woolf was an English novelist regarded as one of the key modernist literary figures of the twentieth century. Her novels include *Mrs. Dalloway* and *To the Lighthouse*.

Nicknames: Gin, Ginny, Ginger, Ginia

W

Wendy: Wendy, Jodi, Lori, Debbie—hey, it's the class of 1985! It's way too soon for a Wendy revival, and not even a sprinkling of fairy dust could get this thirtysomething lady off the ground these days. Speaking of fairy dust, Wendy was invented by J. M. Barrie for his 1904 opus *Peter Pan*.

Before that, it had some mileage as a short form of Gwendolyn. I predict the class of 2085 might take another peek at Wendy—it will take that long for this perky babysitter name to fly into nursery windows again.

Willa: This is truly one of the prettiest, most fabulous, underused names. Willa carries with it both the art-deco stylishness of the thirties, when it was last used quite a bit, and the windblown openness one associates with the prairie settings of Willa Cather's novels. I've heard this only a couple of times lately, but just from the most trailblazing parents. It's like one of those new fashions you see in a magazine, the one that pops out from the other runway offerings and makes you think, "Wow, that *is* gorgeous. Why didn't anyone think to pair those fabrics before?" Cather herself is a noble literary icon, having written such luminous American classics as *My Ántonia* and *O Pioneers*.

> Willa carries with it both the art-deco stylishness of the thirties, when it was last used quite a bit, and the windblown openness one associates with the prairie settings of Willa Cather's novels.

Winnie: Winnie is traditionally the spry little pet form of Winifred, an antique showing signs of restoration. All by itself, Winnie is playful, sweet, and gently old school, kind of like that tubby little cubby, all stuffed with stuff, you know the one I mean. The original Winnie-the-Pooh was named after Winnipeg, the hometown of the World War I soldier who found an orphaned bear cub on his way overseas and donated it to the London Zoo, where it was spotted by A. A. Milne and his son, Christopher Robin. A modern little Winnie would be at home at a tea party (with honey, of course), joining guests Maisie, Fern, and Esmé. A vintage doll with a built-in room décor motif.

Wylie: If you really groove on supertrendy names such as Hayley and Kylie, but don't relish the thought of your daughter sharing her name all the time, have I got a deal for you: Wylie. It sounds just like made-up flash-in-the-pans, but it's an authentic first name and a jaunty Scottish surname. A hundred years ago, it was an uncommon but not unheard of boy's first name. Why not grab it for the girls? In books, Philip Gordon Wylie wrote lots of science fiction novels, including *Gladiator*, which partially inspired Superman, and *When Worlds Collide*, which did spark the comic book character Flash.

Z

Zelda: Aha! A sister name for Binx, Ulysses, Jupiter, and Poe! Okay, so it's not quite that out there, but close. This zesty number kicks it all over the place, so injected as it is with moxie and chutzpah and every other term for cheek and nerve you can think of. Cheeky Robin Williams named his daughter Zelda, apparently after the nervy video game Princess Zelda, whose creator named her after cheeky/ nervy squared Zelda Fitzgerald. This is definitely going to stir the pot, so if the relatives become flustered, advise them to count their blessings: this name started out as Grizelda.

Zola: "Truth is on the march and nothing will stop it," Émile Zola famously said, and that quote captures the candor, veracity, and daring qualities suggested by the name Zola. With ties to Africa, Italy (the writer Zola was ethnically Italian), and France, this is a zesty name that would set any girl up for a lifetime of great expectations. Eddie Murphy must have thought so when he called one of his daughters Zola. Its most famous bearer was an influential French novelist and a major figure in the political liberalization of France.

Zooey: Zooey (rhymes with "gluey"), was actually an affectionate nickname for a boy named Zachary Glass (see Zachary) in Salinger's novella *Franny and Zooey*. Certainly, Zooey would knock their socks off at the PTO, but it's a little too zoological and eccentric for most people. Zoe, in fact, started out in modern-day usage as an idiosyncratic, compact name, long chosen by offbeat parents who wanted something out of the ordinary. At number 30 and rising, Zoe is, unfortunately, no longer a madcap choice, though it's still loveable and cute as can be. For something a bit wilder, check out Zola, Zara, or Zahara. Or even Zooey.

Lorilee's Top 20 Girls' Names

Auden ❊ Beatrix ❊ Esmé ❊ Evangeline ❊ Flannery
❊ Frances ❊ Georgianna ❊ Harper ❊ Josephine ❊ Julia
❊ Lucy ❊ Luna ❊ Marina ❊ Marlowe ❊ May
❊ Nora ❊ Phoebe ❊ Ruby ❊ Tabitha ❊ Violet

Zora: Short of Zoe and Zach, few Z names have ever carved themselves into the mainstream. Why? Most people are very, very safe when it comes to bequeathing an identification on their precious child, and thus Z seems kind of edgy, and maybe a little scary. But the Zs do bustle with energy and enterprise, and Zora in particular crackles with verve. Zora Neale Hurston was an African American writer who was at the center of the Harlem Renaissance of the 1920s with Langston Hughes and Wallace Thurman. She is best known for "Their Eyes Were Watching God." In the Bible, Zorah was a village in Canaan, where God called Samson.

Zora Neale Hurston was an African American writer who was at the center of the Harlem Renaissance of the 1920s with Langston Hughes and Wallace Thurman.

Boys

 A

Abram: While the clunkier Abraham may still sound prohibitively ponderous, Abram sounds more streamlined and accessible in an era where fellow patriarchs Jacob and Isaac are ruling T-ball teams everywhere. In the Bible, Abram was a hero of the faith before and after God added the extra *ha*, to change the meaning of his name from "exalted father" to "father of multitudes." The handle is well used in many great books, including *Romeo and Juliet*, where Abram was a servant of the Montagues. Nicknamewise, Abram is rich: pick either the sporty, honest Abe or the earthy, creative Bram.

Nicknames: Abe, Bram

Ajax: Like Orion, Ajax is a way-out-there possibility that folks will get used to fast. Oh, eyebrows will raise, no doubt about it, but essentially they are already familiar with Ajax because they've been attacking soap scum with it for years. Interestingly, the cleanser's original slogan was "Stronger than dirt," a reference to the mythical character Ajax the Great. He was quite a dude, a burly, brave warrior king who kicked butt all over the Trojan War. If you can get past the product placement—and really, who cares?—this is a tough, slick-sounding name with a flashy nickname: Jax.

Nickname: Jax

Alexander: What's not to like about Alexander? It's urbane and timeless, and people will always be tempted to say "the Great" after uttering it. Clearly, folks have grooved on this strong, warriorlike name (it means "defending warrior") for eons, so the downside here is that it's a top 20 classic. You can refurbish it by going with the abbreviated Xander, which can also shapeshift into Zander or Sander, if you're Dutch. Alexander has popped up all over the great books, including in Shakespeare and as the character Alexander Selkirk in *Robinson Crusoe*.

Nicknames: Alex, Xander, Zander, Sander

Amos: I fail to see why a really old radio show (*Amos 'n Andy*) should have any bearing whatsoever on modern baby naming. Amos is a fabulous thing to be called, a vivid, vigorous name that packs a punch in four letters. You do need a pinch of guts to use it, since it's rare and very old-coot-smoking-a-corncob-pipe-on-the-porch. On the other hand, that's the exact quality that makes it so appealing. In the Old Testament, Amos was the blazing, daring fig farmer who blasted some Israelites for their exploitation of the poor. "Let justice roll on like a river," he roared in Amos

5:24. Amos fits together perfectly with other Bible boys like Jonah, Isaiah, and Elijah. If you have a special burden for justice like the biblical Amos and the literary one—Amos Oz of Israel—this hearty Hebrew name might be for you. Oz, the best-known Israeli writer alive today, is a political activist and the author of nonfiction and fiction, including *My Michael* and *Black Box*.

Angus: It's beefy, clad in plaid, and playing the electric bagpipes—Angus is a Scottish rock star. If you want the world to know you are exuberantly proud of your Highlander roots, by all means, nab Angus. This old-timer-turned-hipster also boasts the fabulous nickname Gus. Did I mention Angus was a rock star? He totally is. In *Macbeth*, Angus was a thane, which means he was a hereditary tenant of the crown.

Nickname: Gus

Anton: Anton is the exchange student from the Baltic Sea who makes all the girls go weak in the knees because he's enigmatic yet sweet. This one's a keeper, folks—it has all the goods to make it a hit with a Slavic flavor that might keep away the lemmings. Anton Chekhov was the medical doctor/playwright/short-story writer who wrote just four plays; every one of them is considered to be an abiding piece of the repertoire. *Uncle Vanya* and *The Cherry Orchard* are perhaps the most famous. Bonus: whether you're Polish, Dutch, Russian, German, or Scandanavian, this name offers an ethnic kicker in an easy-to-spell package. Tony is an old nickname, but in the name of all that is decent, stick with Anton.

Nickname: Tony

Antonio: It's no surprise this sultry name is one favored by daytime dramas. Antonio is all flashing dark brown eyes and mysterious depths of the soul—i.e., it's a swooner. In *Twelfth Night*, for example, Captain Antonio rescues Sebastian from a shipwreck and remains his loyal friend thereafter. Sounds about right. The Bard greatly favored this romantic, Italianate name, dubbing no fewer than five notable characters Antonio.

Archibald/Archer: Part 1: Neglected Old Coot Alert! Let's get past Archie Bunker and his issues and take a fresh look at a grandpa name with plenty of newfangled zip.

Okay, so you might not slap a helpless little kid with a slammer like Archibald, but you can call him Archie or even Arch (a given name with its own history) and call it old-timey cool. The British never had to deal with the Bunkers, so they have always liked this amiable gent. Archibald was the name of a character in *The Secret Garden*. Part 2: So you like Archie but can't quite swallow Archibald? Meet **Archer**. It's a surname, an occupational designation, and it generates the hip grandpa nickname Archie. Wow! This is a steal, a mod hipster with a wise old soul. Grab it while the gettin's good (and if you enjoy taking aim with bows and arrows, your quest for the perfect name may have just ended). Newland Archer was the leading man in Edith Wharton's *The Age of Innocence*.

Nickname: Arch, Archie

If you like Austen, see Archer, Asher, and Anton.

Aristides, Aristotle: Isn't it kind of weighty to name your child after one of the greatest thinkers of all time? Yes, and a lot of pressure too. If you want to aim high, keep in mind that you will be setting your child up for comparisons to someone extremely hard to live up to. (See Romeo and Apollo.) What if the kid turns out to be a philosophy flunkie? (If you're Greek, though, **Aristotle** always works.) **Aristides** is more down-to-earth. In the second century, Aristides the Athenian wrote the influential Christian manifesto called Apology of Aristides. Aris is the uncommonly cool short form for both.

Nickname: Aris

Arthur: When Paul McCartney's first grandchild (born to Mary McCartney) was named Arthur, the Arthurian tide began to turn. Though there have been plenty of Arthurs born in the last century (who, by the way, pretty much all go by Art; modern parents will want to keep the name intact), sometimes it takes a high-profile, turbo baby namer like a Beatle's child to begin the refurbishment of an old classic. If you focus on King Arthur, bronzed and jousting, presiding over the Knights of the Round Table, he seems quite cool. Arthurian legend has been alive since the Middle Ages, and there have been thousands of books and poems about Arthur's valor, including Alfred, Lord Tennyson's *Idylls of the King*.

Asher: Tyler, Hunter, and Parker are all trendy top 100 names, which means everyone is already buttered up for Asher, a fine-looking Old Testament name with loads of

Southern-sounding charm. Ash definitely clicks as a nickname, and sounds like a mannerly Alabaman gentleman drinking iced tea and enchanting the ladies. In the Bible, Asher was the son of Jacob and the leader of one of the twelve tribes of Israel. Chaim Potok's novel *My Name Is Asher Lev*, about an artistic boy growing up in a Hasidic community, is a required-reading favorite in high school.

Nickname: Ash

> **A**tticus Finch displayed moral courage, reason, tolerance, compassion, and uncommon humanity—not a bad set of virtues to affiliate with your child.

Atticus: Many people think of *To Kill a Mockingbird* as their favorite book, remembering that, to their surprise, they couldn't put down this standard required reading of high school English class. One reason is noble Atticus Finch, the fearless attorney who defends an innocent man accused of a heinous crime. This heroic character displayed moral courage, reason, tolerance, compassion, and uncommon humanity—not a bad set of virtues to affiliate with your child. Choosing this Roman name would speak volumes about you: (a) you are an intrepid soul who cares not for the whims of fashion and trendiness, and (b) you care about justice for all. Certainly, Atticus is not for the faint of heart (they would choose Austin). In fact, the name rarely pops up in baby-name books at all. But if you want nothing less than a bold, just, and singular moniker for your singular son, this is for you. Actors Isabella Hoffman and Daniel Baldwin blazed a trail by naming their boy Atticus.

August: This beautiful name means "majestic and venerable," and it is exactly that. August is an old-time gentleman with a European courtliness, perfect for people drawn to Oscar and Max who want something less popular. Actress Mariska Hargitay chose this for her firstborn son, no doubt kicking the name up a few notches. Bonus: two übercool nicknames, Gus and Augie, spring forth from August. Along with Henrik Ibsen, August Strindberg is considered one of the most important Scandinavian writers and one of the fathers of modern theater. He also made a little quip once that stuck: "I dream, therefore I am."

Nicknames: Gus, Augie

Austen: Okay, so maybe a junior Austen won't run around the playground, bragging to Jaden, Caden, and Aiden that he was named after a lady who wrote books with puffed-sleeved heroines on the covers. It's just one letter off from the turbocharged Austin, and no one will know the difference until English lit class, at which point some girl is sure to go wobbly-kneed at how sensitive and dreamy the guy is when he tells her his name's provenance. Until then, this is a trendy ID with a Western kick that's built to last.

Axel: Looking for a name that will set your child up for a lifetime of rock 'n' roll? Ultrahip Axel fits the bill, thanks to Guns N' Roses frontman Axl Rose. This Scandinavian designation (somehow those wild and crazy Swedes got

Axel out of Absalom) is one of the toughest, most muscular names you could possibly choose. It's also unique and straightforward, a combo you don't find every day. Look for an Axel in *The Victory* by Joseph Conrad.

   Nickname: Axe

Balthazar: Balthazar is an enjoyable name to say out loud, but does it have real-world workability? The answer may have been no up until a few years ago, when dashing young actor Balthazar Getty (*Brothers and Sisters*) made his exotic name more familiar. It's quirky but has a decidedly luxurious feel, maybe because Balthazar was the name of one of the three kings of Orient from the nativity story (a Christmas tie-in that could make this a perfect name for a Yule baby). In Shakespeare's *The Comedy of Errors*, Balthazar was a merchant.

Barnaby: Here's a jaunty, friendly ID that will suit all kinds of last names and personalities. Barnaby is pleasingly old-fashioned, but hasn't yet made a dent on the top 1,000. Parents may have shied away because of the obvious nickname Barney, but really, who cares? The full name is good-humored, dashing, and sounds rather British Isles. One can picture a Barnaby having a bag of crisps with his mates Rupert and Seamus before the rugby match. Barnaby Rudge was the title character of Dickens's 1841 historical novel of the Gordon riots of 1780. (Oh, *those* riots of 1780.)

Basil: So it's an herb—why does that matter? It's also a given name with loads of earthy, bohemian charm and quirkiness. This would be the perfect name for a family who drives a hybrid car, lives in a house with solar panels, and wears clothing that is either organic or made of hemp (maybe both). *From the Mixed-Up Files of Mrs. Basil E. Frankweiler* is a novel by E. L. Konigsburg.

Beckett: It just sounds like a rock 'n' roll name, probably because the short form Beck is associated with the Grammy-winning guy with the same name. A punchy, energetic last-name-for-a-first-name, Beckett is a suggestion for the hip, iconoclastic, and inventive among you. Samuel Beckett was an Irish playwright, one of the most rabble-rousing dramatists of the contemporary period. He challenged audiences by peeling away more and more of the conventions associated with theater, experimenting with how far he could go without taking away from the pure essence of the story and the dramatic experience. He is best known for his plays *Waiting for Godot* and *Endgame*.

Nickname: Beck

> Beckett was an Irish playwright, one of the most rabble-rousing dramatists of the contemporary period.

Benjamin: Benjamin is one of the most universally well-liked names, a timeless moniker that harks back to the Old Testament and the patriarchs (Benjamin was Jacob and Rachel's son, the leader of the Benjamite tribe), the genesis of America (Franklin was a founding father), and a classic that will probably endure forever. Like Samuel, Benjamin is still superpopular (on my son's hockey team this year there were three Bens and one Benj), currently ranking at number 24. It's hard to resist Benjamin, obviously, and I can see why. It manages to be strong, masculine, and tender at the same time, plus Ben is an easygoing little short form. If you're looking for a more original golden oldie, check out nonlit choices Reuben (Rube), Josiah, or Levi. If you can't stay away from Benjamin, you're in good company. *The Autobiography of Benjamin Franklin*, the unfinished record of Franklin's life, written from 1771 to 1790, became one of the most famous and influential examples of autobiography ever written.

Nicknames: Ben, Benj, Benji

Bennet: A friend named her son Bennett (with one more *t* than our literary connection) because she loved Ben but didn't care for Benji as a nickname. That's one way to circumvent a hyperpopular name such as Benjamin and still get the nickname you want. Bennet is ten times less used than Benjamin, and it fits in supremely well with the surname rage. If you wanted to mix up the sounds in your kids' names, you could pick Bennet, Preston, and Walker for three different endings but a seamless style match. By the way, my friend doesn't even call her little boy Ben: he's Benny to all. *Pride and Prejudice* aficionados will feel warmly toward Bennet, the last name of beloved Lizzie and her spirited band of sisters.

Nicknames: Benny, Ben

Looking for an alternative to Benjamin? Check out **Bennet**.

Binx: People are naming their children Banjo and Blue, so I say, what about Binx? In *The Moviegoer* by Walker Percy, Binx Bolling was an alienated young stockbroker who found meaning in life when he fought in the Korean War. The novel won the National Book Award in 1962.

Blake: Brisk, cheerful, and a touch urbane, Blake seems like a most trendy and modern name. It's not overused (it hovers between 80 to 100 on the popularity charts), and it would make a handsome choice for parents seeking a cool name that doesn't scream, "Look how hip I am." William Blake was the great English poet and painter whose views of the imagination inspired untold people, especially those who have read his poem "The Marriage of Heaven and Hell." "If the doors of perception were cleansed, everything would appear to man as it is, infinite," he wrote. That's where the Doors got their name.

Booker: Waves of coolness exude from this occupational name for a writer. It's instantly identifiable as the handle of one of the great models of justice and reconciliation:

The Bard's Boys

Abram ❖ Angus ❖ Balthazar ❖ Curran ❖ Duncan
❖ Emmanuel ❖ Griffith ❖ Horatio ❖ Julius ❖ Lennox
❖ Lincoln ❖ Malcolm ❖ Orlando ❖ Orsino ❖ Owen
❖ Philemon ❖ Quintus ❖ Roman ❖ Romeo ❖ Sebastian
❖ Tarquin ❖ Timon ❖ Titus

Booker T. (Taliaferro) Washington. He was the African American educator and author of *Up from Slavery*, his 1901 autobiography, which still resonates today. Still, like Langston, Booker is by no means exclusively African American: it's open to all admirers of the great Booker T. Adding to its bookishness, the Booker Prize is a top literary award.

Bram/Bramwell: A short name that's long on charm, Bram is a cozy, earthy, and handsome name that has its roots as a Dutch variant of Abraham. It definitely has that Euro-cool vibe, plus it's very rarely used. Bram Stoker was the Irishman who penned the 1897 horror classic *Dracula*. If you want to beef up Bram—though it's grand as is—Bramwell was the name of the Brontë sisters' lone brother.

Buck: There are country bumpkin names that can be flipped inside out and sound hip on a city slicker. Buck is not one of them. You may as well call the child Redneck if you're going to call him Buck (Jim Bob, Waylon, and Orville also work in this regard). Buck is the main character—a dog, appropriately enough—in *The Call of the Wild* by Jack London. Pearl S. Buck was a wonderful human being, however, so you may want to wait until you have a girl and name her Pearl in honor of the author of *The Good Earth*.

Byron: Now here's a sturdy, traditional name you don't hear every day. Byron was once a tribute name to Lord Byron, the romantic poet whose real love life made his characters, even Don Juan, seem tame in comparison. Yet Byron as a first name doesn't conjure up swooning ladies or windswept moors. It retains a quietly poetic image, which is probably better than saddling your son with a high-pressure lover-boy handle. (See Romeo.) Although, we've got to give Lord Byron credit for penning those immortal words, "She walks in beauty like the night." There's a line your boy can snag in a romantic situation down the road. (You know, when he's twenty-seven.)

Caleb: It's no wonder Caleb is hot on Jacob, Joshua, Noah, and Ethan's heels as a biblical top 10 phenom. In the book of Joshua, Caleb faced Canaan's giants and his faith held fast. Parents today appreciate this role model, and even those who have never cracked open a Bible find it to be a warm, masculine name with a great meaning: "bold one." Buyer beware, though: Caleb is beautiful but has also passed its freshness date as a nifty find. In Dickens's novella *Cricket on the Hearth*, Caleb Plummer is a poor old toymaker.

Carlo: Boy, I'll tell ya: you just pop an *o* on the end of a name and it's like a makeover on *What Not to Wear*. Carl by itself is rather sedate, but the *o* changes everything. Like tall, dark, and handsome brethren Marco and Antonio, Carlo, the Italian form of Carl, exudes verve and masculinity. This ultra-cool name was borne by Carlo Collodi, or simply Collodi, the creator of Pinocchio, who hailed from Florence, Italy.

Carson/Coleman: Carson is one of those calm, cool, and collected customers that sounds absolutely smashing with a huge variety of last names. It's smooth (thanks to

"Heeeeere's Johnny" Carson) *and* rustic, courtesy of Wild West cowboy Kit. I prefer it to top 100 mainstay Carter, actually, because the "son" ending is a little less trendy and less used. **Coleman** is about six times less popular than Carson, and yields a can't-beat-it, two-for-one deal with the well-liked Cole as a nickname. Coleman, by the way, adds depth and substance to Cole, which, standing alone, seems rather slight. Both Carson and Coleman are well-built, good-looking surnames with solid literary keystones: Carson McCullers was the Southern author of such classics as *The Heart Is a Lonely Hunter* (an Oprah Book Club pick, which revived its readership considerably), and Billy Coleman was the winsome young boy at the heart of Wilson Rawls's *Where the Red Fern Grows*.

> Love top 100 mainstay Carter? Check out Carson and Coleman for less trendy alternatives.

Nickname: Cole

Chandler: A nineties success story that spiked along with the hyperpopularity of TV's *Friends*. Now that the show is in syndication—and Matthew Perry has moved on to other things—Chandler sounds less like a vibrant, fresh choice with a sense of humor and more like a prep-school kid in a uniform. It's already sliding down the chart as fast as you can say "Central Perk." *Ch* names with more vitality include Cheever, Chauncey, and Chester, not to mention classic Charlie. Raymond Thornton Chandler introduced the hard-boiled detective archetype in his crime novels starring the cynical Philip Marlowe.

Charles: You can't go wrong with Charles, one of the most noble and venerable names in all of history (since Charlemagne, anyway). Yes, it's been popular for ages—literally—and remains in the top 100 (in the form of Charlie), but back in the sixties and seventies, people turned this stately creature into Chuck. (There should be an emoticon for shuddering.) No one does that anymore. Instead, Charlie is a cozy, amiable nickname that goes incredibly well with Sam and Max and Ben, et al. Charles belonged to many literary geniuses, including Charles Dickens.

Nickname: Charlie

Cheever: It's a surname, a maverick, and totally unique: meet Cheever. Think of this as a cross between Charlie and Carter, with a little Keaton thrown in, and maybe it will start to seem more viable. Certainly, there is now widespread acceptance of last names in the first slot, and people will soon warm up to Cheever's jovial vibe. John Cheever was an American novelist and short-story writer who wrote keenly observed tales of suburban life. His *The Stories of John Cheever* won the Pulitzer Prize for fiction in 1979.

Chester: A century ago, Chester was a top 100 name, so it stands to reason this old coot could make a comeback. (So far it hasn't.) I think it has potential, not only because it's old-timey and cozy (can't you just see a Chester in a cuddly flannel shirt?), but because it has the totally hip nickname Chet (as in Atkins, the legendary country guitar player). Plus Tom Hanks and Rita Wilson have a son named Chester (and how cool are they?). G. K. (Gilbert Keith) Chesterton was an influential English writer of the early twentieth century and a member of C. S. Lewis's Inklings. He was the author of *Orthodoxy*, considered a religious classic by many.

   Nickname: Chet

Clive: A veddy, veddy British name, Clive won't be most folks' cup of tea, but it does have a current redeemer in the form of hottie actor Clive Owen. Still, I'm thinking Clive won't receive quite the same bounce as Jude did when Jude Law came on the scene. It's a bit too upper-crust and unapproachable, like, say, Jeeves and Niles. However, it does have a unique sound, and the right family might be able to pull it off. Clive Staples, or C. S. Lewis, as he was known, authored the beloved Chronicles of Narnia series, among other enduring books.

Conan: Has this name been completely overlooked because of a 1982 flick that gave Arnold Schwarzenegger his breakthrough role? Well, that's just silly at this point. It's actually a hot little name with lots of muscle and vigor. (Okay, so that might be Arnold's influence.) Conan was an Irish saint, is a superfly talk show host, and was also one of the names of the purveyor of the Sherlock Holmes mysteries, Sir Arthur Conan Doyle.

Conrad: An intriguing, tough name with some serious Eastern European heft, this one lines up well with Euro-flavored kin Anton, Johann, and Hugo. Conrad is also burlier than Connor, and way less trendy. Con is the obvious nickname, but how many names can you legitimately wrangle Rad out of? That's kind of cool, when you think about it.

Joseph Conrad (born Teodor Józef Konrad Korzeniowski) was the ethnically Polish British novelist of such works as *Lord Jim* and *Heart of Darkness*.

Nicknames: Con, Rad

Cooper: Once upon a time, coopers were guys who built chicken dwellings for a living. Since then the name has skewed upwards from its humble origins, becoming rather neo-yuppie. The amiable Coop ultimately saves it from being too preppie. James Fenimore Cooper was, of course, the American romantic writer of such frontiersman sagas as *The Last of the Mohicans* and *The Deerslayer*.

Nickname: Coop

Cormac: Let's face it, Aidan is at the peak of the popularity chart, Connor is a top 20 fixture, and Liam is climbing its way up. We need some new Irish faces, and Cormac is just that: a fresh, amiable, and singular name just waiting to be plucked by parents with a pinch of boldness. *Somehow*, and don't ask me how this happened, but Cormac has yet to crack the top 1,000, despite a legion of readers being familiar with the name via major American novelist Cormac McCarthy. There's a head scratcher for you. But don't think about it too much. Just snag Cormac and make a dash for the delivery room.

Nickname: Mac

Curran: Sick of Connor? Tired of Cameron? Like Liam, Curran is cut from a new, more identifiably Irish bolt of cloth, but unlike Liam (now a top 100 name), Curran is as fresh as a pint of Guinness in a pub. Meaning "hero, champion," this is

Grab Curran and run—people are on a rampage for Irish boys' names, and Liam will sound new only for so long.

a name with some spice that works very well in the real world. I would grab this one and run, because people are on a rampage for Irish boys' names, and Liam can only sound new for so long. Curan was a character in *King Lear*.

Daniel: Evergreen Daniel is as old as the Old Testament hero who faced the lion's den and as new as yesterday's crop of baby boys at your local hospital. At this point, as it seems to have squatting rights to the number 7 spot on the list, Daniel is not among your wild and wacky options, but parents who choose it are much more concerned about its venerability and can't-go-wrong sensibility. It's a pure classic, and as such, it turns up in a library's worth of pages, including on the frontispiece of Daniel Defoe's *Robinson Crusoe*, a tale of a shipwrecked castaway who faces mutineers, savages, and wild animals before being rescued. *Crusoe* inspired Swift's *Gulliver's Travels*, which, parenthetically, was Daniel Boone's favorite book.

Dante: Well used in the African American community, Dante is a lush old Italian contraction of Durante. Dante is tall, dark, and handsome, smart, and a little exotic. Durante Degli Alighieri, better known as Dante, was an Italian poet from Florence whose *Divina Commedia* (*The Divine Com-*

edy), is considered one of the greatest masterpieces of world literature.

Darby: A cheerful, animated Irishman's name that would suit a smiley young boy wonderfully well (and, it must be said, would be perfect for a chipper young girl as well). Right now, though, with Patrick Dempsey naming one of his twin boys Darby Dempsey, the status quo has tilted firmly toward the boys—for now. Darby O'Gill was the whistling bloke who appears in the writings of the Irish American author Herminie Templeton Kavanagh, including *Darby O'Gill and the Good People*.

Dashiell: This is possibly the coolest boys' name in the book, an old-timey hipster that has all the swagger and polish of a 1930s detective novel. Think Humphrey Bogart in *The Maltese Falcon* and you're getting awfully close to the wry, urbane spirit of the name, borne by Dashiell Hammet, the creator of hardboiled PIs Sam Spade and Nick and Nora Charles. Actress Cate Blanchett named her little boy Dashiell, and the moniker got another big shot of juice when it was used on the zippy little superhero Dashiell Parr (known as Dash) of *The Incredibles*. So let's tally up the pros here—art deco panache, celebrity pick, fabulous animated movie tie-in—and we're talking name perfection. (Pssst: Between you and me, Dashiell hasn't even cracked the top 1,000 yet, so it's also highly original. Can you speak? No, me neither. I can only blither.) Make a mad dash for this swanky fella and you'll be glad you did.
    Nickname: Dash

Dexter: It's a bird, it's a plane, it's Dexter, a hot yet nerdy name that pulls off hotness and nerdiness in one fell swoop. This makes it ultracool, because all the hippest people are riding that razor's edge between being fabulous and being goofy (and they remain fabulous because they are okay with that colorful splash of goofiness, like new parents of a Dexter, Diana Krall and Elvis Costello). Dexter will definitely be in a band someday, and he will probably play the upright bass. And truly, you can hardly come up with a slicker trim job than Dex. That final *x* is smoking hot. Dexter Green was a character in Fitzgerald's short story "Winter Dreams."

> It's a bird, it's a plane, it's Dexter, a hot yet nerdy name that pulls off hotness and nerdiness in one fell swoop.

Nickname: Dex

Doyle: Usually I can step out of preconceived ideas I have had about various names. The nasty, hulking kid I once knew who nearly ruined a certain trendy name for me, or the uptight English teacher from grade eight who tainted a certain Victorian revival for all time—I have learned to look at even those emotionally loaded names with some detachment. I can't detach from Doyle, because I've been married to him for fifteen years, and he is all I can see when I try to evaluate his name. He is also insistent that I include this name in the book, because, as he points out, it *is* Sir Arthur Conan Doyle's last name, and I did use Conan. So here goes: *Doyle is a spectacular name, an unusually handsome and powerful name that will stand your child in good stead for the rest of his life.* That's my official statement on the matter.

Unofficially, however, it's an old-fangled, highly uncommon name that happens to be one of those all-popular Irish surnames. It could work. But—sorry, dear—I still like Conan the teensiest little bit better.

DuBois: Here's a fascinating idea for a first or middle name, although "statement" names tend to go better in that middle slot. People have used family names such as DuPont and DuPree as middle names, so why not honor a great author and activist? W. E. B DuBois (pronounced "doo-BOYZE") wrote *The Souls of Black Folk* in 1903. It was considered a foundational text for the civil rights movement.

Duncan: It seems everywhere one looks these days people are trying to get in touch with their Celtic roots, what with all the boys named Liam, Colin, and Aiden running around. Check out Duncan, a kingly appellation that sounds just right for the Brandon/Jackson/Ethan set but is hundreds of miles from those names in terms of usage. Duncan was a noble king of Scotland, unfortunately offed in his bed by Macbeth in Shakespeare's play of the same name.

Dylan: Twenty years ago, Dylan carried a certain romantic, brooding image, a rebellious yet high-minded blend of Bob Dylan's status-quo-challenging lyrics and Dylan Thomas's luminous poetry. All of these rich benefits were seriously diluted by the onset of *Beverly Hills, 90210*, when an entire generation began to think of one person and one person only: the brooding, romantic, status-quo-challenging character Dylan McKay. The show single-handedly catapulted the name Dylan to the top 30, where it stands today. Still, with the show now off the air for several years, perhaps conventional wisdom will once again regard Dylan in the literary context that is rightfully his. Dylan Thomas, who wrote, among his many poems, "A Child's Christmas in Wales," only and always aspired to be a poet, enclosed as he was in his own private world of words. He was once quoted as saying, "When I experience anything I experience it as a thing and word at the same time." Meaning "from the sea," this Welsh handle was chosen in recent years by actors at opposite ends of the image spectrum: Pierce Brosnan and Pamela Anderson (sorry, did I give you whiplash?), and more recently by Michael Douglas and Catherine Zeta-Jones.

Edgar: Take the image of a stuffy English butler, and turn it inside out. What do you have? A name that is so unbearably antiquated it could easily be hip again. (Who thought ten years ago Gus and Oscar would have another shot at style?) And because of the lit namesake here, Edgar Allan Poe, it's a bit gothic around the edges, dark and mysterious, yet with a sneaky sense of humor. It's more offbeat by far than Edward, and for some folks, that's a good thing.

Elias: Here's a magnificent name that sounds more handsome every time you say it. Elias, the Greek form of Elijah, is slowly making inroads amongst arbiters of taste with its striking good looks and magnetism. Eli is a feasible nickname, too, making this a nifty two-for-one deal.

Elias Canetti was a German-speaking Jew from a long line of Sephardic Jews, originally from Spain (where his family got their last name). His books were all written in German, and in 1981 he won the Nobel Prize in literature.

Nickname: Eli

Eliot: Rarely in this business are we blown away by names that should be well used, but are somehow rare. Eliot is one, with its zenith moment thus far having been cracking the top 1,000 in the 1960s, as number 1,000 (although the Elliot spelling hangs out in the 300s on the current list). Eliot sounds like an intense poetry major with a shy smile that causes his fellow poetry majors to forget all about Keats and Yeats. It should be noted, though it should not cause alarm, that Eliot is being used somewhat for girls. Poet T. S. Eliot wrote myriad poems, including "The Love Song of J. Alfred Prufrock."

Ellis/Ellison: Here's a somewhat novel surname idea cut from the same cloth as Jackson and Sullivan. If you're looking for an *E* name that is not as overblown as Evan or Ethan, Ellis is quiet yet strong, classy but still cool, and also has special meaning for those whose forebears came through Ellis Island en route to new lives as Americans. Emily Brontë originally published *Wuthering Heights* under the pseudonym Ellis Bell. Bonus: it's hard to wrangle a nickname out of Ellis, if you're looking for something that won't be shortened by anyone. However, if a longer name is what you hanker for, check out **Ellison.** Ralph Waldo Ellison, named by his father after Ralph Waldo Emerson, was the African American author of *Invisible Man*.

Emerson: Emerson sounds like someone to be taken seriously. It's a noble appellation with historical and literary underpinnings, but still has a modern ring to it. In the wake of Jackson, Christian, and Landon—all old-fashioned surnames—hitting the big time, the time is ripe for Emerson to charge ahead likewise. Ralph Waldo Emerson was a poet, essayist, and orator. His *Essays: First and Second Series*, is considered to be one of the one hundred greatest books of all time.

Emmanuel: Emmanuel is a beautiful, handsome, and weighty name that could make a distinctive first or middle name choice for a Christmas baby. (It means "God with us.") This one has broad appeal across ethnic lines, having been appropriated by parents of all backgrounds, including Jewish, African American, and Hispanic. Emmanuel was a character in Shakespeare's *Henry IV, Part 2*.

Nickname: Manny

Ernest: Earnestness does not go out of style, even if the name Ernest is currently dusted over. In Oscar Wilde's play *The Importance of Being Earnest*, a character said, "There is something in that name that seems to inspire absolute confidence. I pity any poor woman whose husband is not named Ernest." (My husband's middle name is Ernest, does that count?) You could look at this oldie as a new virtue name, like True or Noble or Justice. To me, it conveys sincerity and industriousness, not bad qualities to have in your name these days. I know: it's old and clunky sounding, but the right pair could blow the dust off this puppy and turn it into a retro-cool, geeky-hip name. Ernie is also giving off oddly cute vibes, as of about five minutes ago. You could also honor Ernest Hemingway, "Papa," one of the greatest writers America has ever produced.

Ethan: You've got to hand it to the Puritans. They had the panache and good sense to launch such unheard-of gems as Ethan, and many parents have followed in their footsteps, especially in recent years. Ethan has a dual image, as a scholarly young man on the rowing team at Yale and as a wrangler swapping stories around the campfire. Edith Wharton's troubled title character, Ethan Frome, injects some literary feel, while Revolutionary War soldier Ethan Allen (of furniture fame) lends historic backbone. Ethan also pops up in the Bible a couple of times, most notably as the grandson of Judah. At this point, it's number 3, and perhaps headed for top spot, so it's not exactly a daring choice.

Evan: In 2006, it seemed like everyone I knew was naming their babies Evan, so I wasn't surprised to see this Welsh form of John crack the top 30 that year. Parents love the soft yet rugged sound, an appealing Ethan/Ryan hybrid that goes well with lots of last names. Of course, with great appeal often comes great popularity, and with that, a commonality that dilutes the essential worth of the name. Looking for an *E* name with more sizzle? Try Emmett, Ezra, or Elias. Evan S. Connell is an American novelist who is best known for *Mrs. Bridge* and *Mr. Bridge*.

Like Evan and Ethan? Emmett, Ezra, and Elias have more sizzle.

Evelyn: Talk about a Boy Named Sue. Evelyn ("Eve-lyn") Waugh, British author of such novels as *Brideshead Revisited*, was once called a "first-rate comic genius." It makes sense; maybe he needed a sense of humor to get through life with a girlie-mon name like Evelyn. His given name was Arthur, though, which makes his choice to go by his middle name quite the head scratcher.

Ezra: As the mother of an Ezra, I can truly give it a ringing endorsement. It's idiosyncratic—in a good way—creative, tough, poetic, and bold. You'll call him Ez, too, which has plenty of zip. One unexpected bonus for me was the pleasure of introducing my Ezra to the gorgeously illustrated books of Ezra Jack Keats. The Caldecott-winning artist and children's book author acquainted untold kiddies with Peter, the star of such classics as *A Snowy Day*. That Peter was black phased many people in the day (1950s and '60s), but not Keats: "My book would have him there simply because he should have been there all along," he said of his choice to have a main black character, not just a token figure. Poet Ezra Pound, naturally, is a huge lit star, and the biblical Ez was a great leader and a scribe as well. And one more thing: Gregory Peck played Ezra Baxter in the film adaptation of Marjorie Kinnan Rawlings's *The Yearling*.

Nickname: Ez

Finn: I fell in love with this name in high school, when it first popped onto my radar in the form of an übercool

German exchange student bearing this tag. He played classical guitar, wore beautiful wool sweaters, and generally radiated waves of Euro-coolness. Since then, of course, the name is a full-fledged superstar: it's attached to a former *Grey's Anatomy* character (played by Chris O'Donnell, who incidentally has a little Finley) and is the everyday ID of Julia Roberts's boy twin, Phinneaus. And who is more laid-back, congenial, and bumpkin-cool than Mr. Huckleberry Finn? Bonus: If you have Irish roots and are sick of Aidan/Colin/Liam, Finn is Fab-oo. Actor Ed Burns and wife Christy Turlington thought so, and Finn Burns is the result.

Finnegan: Vibrantly Irish, Finnegan is not only a lengthening of the hugely appealing Finn, but also a cool full name with its own literary heritage. Rooted in the street ballad of the same name, *Finnegans Wake* was James Joyce's final novel, one which took him twenty-two years to write. If you love Finn but find it too short, your answer is the cheery Finnegan, which goes spectacularly well with such Celtic last names as O'Malley, Healey, Kavanaugh, et al. A stupendous choice.

Fitzwilliam/Fitzgerald: I've often wondered if Lizzie called her beloved Mr. Darcy or Fitzwilliam after they got hitched and settled into happily ever after. Certainly, he was hardly referred to by his first name in all of *Pride and Prejudice*. It was his mother's maiden name, which makes Fitzwilliam a possible candidate for restoration in this surname-crazed era. Maybe. Fitzwilliam Darcy certainly was a swoon-worthy romantic hero, wasn't he? Fitz could

I've often wondered if Lizzie called her beloved Mr. Darcy or Fitzwilliam after they got hitched and settled into happily ever after. Certainly, he was hardly referred to by his first name in all of *Pride and Prejudice*.

work as a zippy short form, for both Fitzwilliam and **Fitzgerald,** if you want to honor F. Scott, the author of *The Great Gatsby*.

Fletcher: If you're looking for something off the beaten path yet not wacky, Fletcher combines the strength of an old tradesman name with an idiosyncratic sound. The result is a true individual who charts his own trail (and perhaps one day makes his own arrows too). Fletch is a cheerful nickname, even if you take Chevy Chase out of the equation. Beaumont and Fletcher (Francis Beaumont and John Fletcher) were a playwriting team that wrote some fifty-five plays during the reign of James I, including *Cupid's Revenge* and *The Maid's Tragedy*.

Nickname: Fletch

Forster: A hybrid of Foster and Forrest, Forster could make a galant, old-school surname choice that would almost be completely one of a kind. E. M. (Edward Morgan) Forster was an early-twentieth-century writer whose novels, including *Howard's End*, *A Room with a View*, and *A Passage to India*, have nearly all been made into films.

Frank: To be candid, this name sounded great-uncle-ish until about ten minutes ago, when pop culture mavens Diana Krall and Elvis Costello conferred it upon one of their twin sons. (Frankie Costello. Is it just me or does that name give you shivers—good shivers?) It was a blockbuster hit around 1900, which means oodles of you have a Frank in your family tree someplace. It's time to pluck off this old-timer and honor Great-Uncle Frank. Or, go with it just because you get a kick out Frank's upfront, what-you-see-is-what-you-get sensibility. Our lit idol for this one? L. (Lyman) Frank Baum, pop culture maven of a century ago and author of *The Wonderful Wizard of Oz*. Frankie is supercute for a little boy, too.

Franklin: Franklin has a real shot at some upward mobility in the near future. Parents who like surnames such as Jackson and Carson may also be searching for something less trendy. Frank is always a player, but it's quite blunt and plain, too. Franklin spruces up Frank and makes it more approachable, plus it's presidential and attached to the great Benjamin Franklin—not a bad lineage at all. Bonus: a little Franklin today will have a special bond with the cute, hockey-playing turtle of TV fame and the children's books by Paulette Bourgeois. Check out J. D. Salinger's short story "Just Before the War with the Eskimos" to read about a character named Franklin.

Frederick: If Max, Gus, Oscar, and even Arthur are experiencing a resurgence, I don't see how Frederick can stay in the fashion doldrums for much longer. It's a fine old name, with much to recommend it, including a stellar name-model in the form of the powerful orator and abolitionist Frederick Douglass. His best-known work was his autobiography, *Narrative of the Life of Frederick Douglass, an American Slave*, which drew ire because critics could not believe such a fluent and erudite piece of literature could have been written by a black man. If you have a much admired and loved family member named Fred, don't be afraid to swipe it off the family tree and use it. Frederick, Fred, and Freddie are all companionable with today's hot old-coot names.

Nicknames: Fred, Freddie

Fritz/Franz: A pet name of Frederick, Fritz could fly with parents searching for a Dutch/German/Swiss name with plenty of ethnic zip. It's a happy name, full of beans—a refreshing change of pace from all the superserious names out there. Fritz peaked in popularity during the 1890s, probably in correlation with the influx of European immigrants that streamed into the country then. Book lovers know Fritz as the gentle German immigrant, Professor Friedrich Bhaer, to whom Jo March lost her heart in *Little Women*. Both Fritz and **Franz** (and Ernst) were shipwrecked on a deserted island in the East Indies with their kin, the Swiss Family Robinson, where they lived in a tree house, fought snakes and pirates, and generally behaved infinitely better than any of the cast members of *Survivor*.

Frodo: Frodo is a Danish king's name, and a very cool sounding appellation, but is only suitable for the most rabid

Celtic Chaps

Angus ❖ Beckett ❖ Conan ❖ Cormac ❖ Curran ❖ Darby
❖ Doyle ❖ Duncan ❖ Finn/Finnegan ❖ Lennox ❖ Lucan
❖ Mulligan ❖ O'Casey ❖ O'Neill ❖ Seamus ❖ Yeats

Lord of the Rings fan. Frodo, as all *Rings* fans know, was the hero of the whole shebang, a hobbit who was also known as the Ring Bearer. I've heard people use this for their dogs, and until we reach the third age, that might be the way to go.

Frost: This is one of those surnames-as-first-names that will play infinitely better in the South, where folks have been making use of family designations such as Harper, Carson, and Flannery for hundreds of years. The poetic choice (obviously) pays tribute to Robert Frost, whose most famous work was the gentle "Walking by the Woods on a Snowy Evening." Your last name should ideally be something more off the beaten path, because Frost paired with a common Anderson or Baker will almost certainly make people think "law firm." If someone makes a remark about Frosty the Snowman, well, they might have a point. Better used, then, in clement weather zones.

G

Gabriel: During your son's turbulent toddler years, you can comfort yourself with the thought that you named him after an angel. Perhaps someday he will live up to the peace and composure that suggests! Gabriel is a poet, the shy guy in Hispanic lit with great hair and a crooked smile. Though not the toughest name on the block (see Conan), Gabriel is hardly wimpy either. With a hale and hearty short form like Gabe, your kid can confidently check fellow sporty dudes Jake and Nick into the boards at a hockey game. Gabriel was an archangel who appeared to, among others, Mary, when he announced she would give birth to the son of God. Other well-known bearers include Gabriel Fahrenheit and Gabriel García Márquez, author of *Love in the Time of Cholera*.

Nickname: Gabe

George: Good old George was a top 5 smash hit for over fifty years, until folks started thinking it sounded fuddy-duddy and began appointing their blue-blanketed bundles with such flashy upstarts as Lloyd and Dick. But here's the thing: after 110 years, names start to sound mighty fresh again, and parents recycle their great-grandparents' oldies (acting, of course, like they came up with the idea in the first place). George is presidential and literary (George Bernard Shaw was the great Irish playwright who penned, among other plays, *Pygmalion* and *Candida*). Jimmy Stewart's George Bailey taught us that no man is a failure when he has friends. And Curious George regaled us all with tales of swinging from vines, munching on bananas, and snooping into every conceivable situation. At any rate, George isn't fusty anymore. It has the same cozy, one-syllable cachet as Gus, Hank, and Max, and a supermodel (Eva Herzigova) dubbed her baby thus. (Supermodels have a knack for being ahead of the trends. See Johan.) And Geo? Now that's slick.

Nickname: Geo

Gideon: Gideon brandishes a fearless, muscular impression. This robust name, which means "destroyer, feller of trees," would suit an intrepid two-year-old as well as a brave grown-up man. In the Bible, Gideon courageously defeats the evil Midianites, so if you're looking for a bold, out of the ordinary biblical name, this one rocks. Actor Mandy Patinkin has a son named Gideon, which was also the name of his character on *Criminal Minds*. *Little Women* fans may recall that Gideon March was the dear papa of Meg, Jo, Beth, and Amy, a scholar and minister who served as a chaplain in the Union Army.

Gilbert: Ever since Gilbert Blythe called his future paramour Anne Shirley "Carrots" (and she broke a slate over his head), he has lent a certain dash of quiet romanticism to his staid name. Of course, *Anne of Green Gables* was written more than a hundred years ago, and though it was considered sleek and urbane then, Gilbert's moniker has since taken a nosedive in popularity. But it's those kinds of "are they geeky or are they cool?" names that indeed sound oddly hip. I'm talking about Walter, Lewis, Phinnaeus, and Homer. Gil, Gib, and Gibby are all established short forms.

Nicknames: Gil, Gib, and Gibby

Graham: This is a cozy, well-built, good-looking name that somehow never caught fire on this side of the ocean (unlike similar hotties Ian and Gavin). I say, don't ask questions, just grab this goody and run! Graham has the nice advantage of not being the least bit trendy, like fellow Scottish/English names Keegan or Colin. Graham Greene wrote travel essays, short stories, plays, and novels, including *The Power and the Glory* and *The End of the Affair*.

Griffith: If folks got used to Kenneth en masse, surely they will warm to Griffith, which, though a little harder to say than Griffin, is also quite a bit more rare. The Welsh, who gave us Dylan and Jennifer and Gwyneth (and many more), are also the source of **Griffith.** He was a gentleman usher to Queen Katharine in Shakespeare's *Henry VIII*. Griff is a fun little nickname, too.

    Nickname: Griff

Gulliver: If you can think of Gulliver as a stylistic cross between Sullivan and Oliver, this vigorous name might sound a little more plausible. It connotes the same kind of thrilling escapades, playfulness, and questing as Gulliver from Jonathan Swift's 1735 epic *Gulliver's Travels: Travels into Several Remote Nations of the World*, a story about Lemuel Gulliver's journeys to Lilliput and other dreamscape lands. It's an original possibility in this age of surnames, especially bubbly Irish ones. Actor Gary Oldman must agree: he named his son Gulliver.

Gus: Should Oscar, Max, Ruby, and Frances need a name for their baby brother, look no further than Gus. Or, if you don't want to have five kids, just use this zesty, fun tag the first time, especially if you like short, punchy names such as Sam and Liv. To give it more versatility, how about giving a more formal designation up front? Angus and Gustave (as in Flaubert, the great French novelist and writer of *Madame Bovary*) both work. This is another one of those mensch monikers—see Oscar, Harry, Leo—that sound so hip these days.

Harper: Harper crosses gender lines easily, even though the most famous bearer, author Harper Lee of *To Kill a Mockingbird*, is female. Paul Simon named his son Harper years ago, and long before that, at the end of the nineteenth century, it was used exclusively for boys. It's a smashing thing to be called for a boy or a girl.

Harry: Harry's old MO was as someone's grandpa, smoking a pipe while reclining in a Barcalounger, with slippers delivered on cue by the dog. Enter Prince Harry, who grew up in front of us and lent his oldster name some serious red-haired cuteness and likeability. Then...drumroll please: Harry Potter swooped in on a bookish broomstick and injected the name with major juice for the conceivable future. Now Harry sounds cool, adventuresome, earnest, and snappy and it shares old-coot stylishness with Leo and Oscar. Harry Morgan was also a character in Hemingway's *To Have and Have Not*.

Hawkins/Hawthorne: Here are two *Haw* names with very different images. First, there's Hawthorne, a very august and ponderous name, drenched in a library's worth of evocations and literary pedigree. Most parents would consider this to be too daunting a name to pull off, even for the biggest fans of Nathaniel Hawthorne, author of *The Scarlet Letter* and

The House of Seven Gables. Still, soap opera characters have borne the short form Thorne, so there may be some useability here. **Hawkins**, on the other hand, is more functional. Hawk is a nature name that suggests soaring and all that jazz, and it could play well on the playground—it sounds like a gutsy kid no one wants to mess with. In *Treasure Island*, Jim Hawkins, who goes by Hawkins, was the young man who finds the treasure map and is the narrator for most of the story.

Heath, Heathcliff: Heath is a breezy, masculine name with a great nature connection. (Heath is low-growing, woody vegetation.) The late Heath Ledger's mother named him Heathcliff because she loved the Brönte character. For true literary lineage, consider Heathcliff, which if you plan on using wholly, is another thing altogether. One can look at this name two ways: as either the archetypical tortured romantic hero of *Wuthering Heights* or as the archetypical happy-dad hero, Dr. Heathcliff Huxtable, from *The Cosby Show*.

> Heathcliff can be looked at as either the archetypical tortured Romantic hero of *Wuthering Heights*, or as the archetypical happy-dad hero, Dr. Heathcliff Huxtable, from *The Cosby Show*.

Henry: Regal, historically rich Henry has recently popped into the top 100, no surprise to anyone who admires its brainy good looks. A pure classic, Henry has been worn by any number of kings and also by a current British prince, who goes by Harry. Henrys on book covers include Henry James, Henry Wadsworth Longfellow, and Henry David Thoreau—not a bad gang to hook up with. Don't ask me how, but Hank is also an acceptable nickname (makes about as much sense as Harry) and lends some baseball cachet, due to the great Mr. Aaron. Julia Roberts's third child is Henry.

Holden: Holden is poised for big things. Though not nearly as overheated as Hayden, Logan, or Hunter, Holden is drawing parents with its modern sound and handsome good looks. This name is elegant but not fake, probably due to the phony-repellent Holden Caulfield of *Catcher in the Rye* fame. Because his character resonates to this day with countless readers, Holden is a name people will warm to quickly. It's definitely on the rise, but it may always be one of those treasures, bypassed by the masses yet loved by a few. *The Catcher in the Rye* was written by J. D. Salinger in 1951.

> Like Hayden, Logan, and Hunter? Handsome Holden is a lot less popular.

Homer: Like stigma busters Richard Gere and Anne Heche, who chose this name for their sons in a world where most folks think Homer is yellow and "D'oh"-y, I say yes to this most unconventional option. It's fantastically literary, with the eighth-century BC epic poet to back it up, but thanks to Mr. Simpson and his wide-eyed ilk, it doesn't take itself too seriously. If this homey, quirky-cool tag appeals to you, be bold and go forth into uncharted lands, like the heroes of Homer's *The Illiad* and *The Odyssey*.

Horatio: A gusty, audacious choice, Horatio is best known for being attached to men of the sea, such as the fictional

A is for *Atticus*

Homer is fantastically literary, with the eighth century BC epic poet to back it up, but thanks to Mr. Simpson and his wide-eyed ilk, it doesn't take itself too seriously.

Horatio Hornblower (of the Age of Sail novels by C. S. Forester), and Vice Admiral Horatio Nelson, one of England's greatest naval heroes. Fiction's sailor man was actually named after Shakespeare's landlubber, Horatio, a well-liked character who served as Hamlet's scholarly friend and confidant. David Caruso brings a modern edge with his portrayal of a Horatio on *CSI: Miami*.

Huckleberry: Give 'em the berries and choose this wildly adventurous literary name, connected now and always with the eponymous Huckleberry Finn. This rather outlandish name got a big shot in the arm when country star Brad Paisley and his wife, actress Kimberley Williams-Paisley, named their son William Huckleberry. They introduced the idea of using Huckleberry in the middle slot, the perfect place for such a renegade. The allusion to one of the great characters in American fiction instantly evokes homemade rafts floating down the Mississippi River, freedom, and boyhood escapades. Commenting on the brouhaha over their name choice, Brad Paisley weighed in: "Huckleberry Finn [is] a reference to a spirit of adventure I hope he embodies. I can see him now—out playing in the woods, taking chances. Sorta conjures up ideas of Mark Twain, you know." We do know, and it's pretty darn cool.

Hugo/Hugh: Hugo, a vigorous, attractive name that may be more popular than you think, is ascending quietly, especially among Latino families. But the name isn't hyper-identifiable as such, like Miguel or Pedro. Hugo could be Pan-European, German, Spanish, or French, like the famous bearer Victor Hugo of *Les Misérables* and *The Hunchback of Notre-Dame* fame. Debonair Hugo is attached to rock-solid, historical Hugh—the *o* ending just makes it pop. **Hugh** isn't quite as charismatic as Hugo, projecting a more reserved and stately vibe that's even a bit posh. Hugh Grant's rakish grin gives the name a big boost. *The Story of Dr. Doolittle*, about the beloved medical man from Puddleby-on-the-Marsh, was written by Hugh Lofting.

Humphrey: Humphrey is one of those names that is so quirky, out-of-fashion, and unheard-of that it could sound stellar on the right kid. Of course, silver-screen icon Bogart adds a glamorous, gruff sheen with his unforgettable "Here's looking at you, kid" persona. Humphrey Van Weyden, a main character in Jack London's *The Sea-Wolf*, becomes a castaway twice and escapes to a deserted island with his shipboard love. A cool story, but the character has a dubious nickname: Hump.

Iago: Othello's ultra-creepy, sinister, nasty piece of work (you get the picture) has unfortunately tainted this name—perhaps until the end of civilization.

Ian: Every woman I know loves the name Ian. It just sounds like a rakishly charming gent with a twinkle in his eye. It's an

especially princely addition to a plaid surname such as Mac-
Gregor or Gilroy (one of the best-named individuals I ever
met was a guy named Ian MacBeth). Still, Ian has been done
quite a bit; there may be room for only a few more before
it hits its saturation point. Ian Lancaster Fleming's *Casino
Royale* was his first novel featuring secret agent James Bond.
He also wrote *Chitty Chitty Bang Bang* for his son Caspar.

Ibsen: If you are a passionate theater lover, or of Norwegian descent, or both, here's an extremely novel, fascinating choice. This belonged to Henrik Ibsen, arguably the
father of modern drama, and the great playwright behind
such thespian showcases as *A Doll's House* and *Hedda
Gabler*. With ethnic names revving up, Scandinavians are reaching back into their ancestries for Nils, Lars, Anders, and Villem (I even know one Viking). If you want to take it a step (or five) beyond those goodies, take a chance on this fantastically creative and evocative name.

> If you are a passionate theater lover, Ibsen is an extremely novel, fascinating choice.

Isaac: Isaac was the original miracle baby who came in
the sunset of Abraham and Sarah's life together. He joins
fellow patriarch Jacob in the top 100 (though he's still far
behind in the rankings) as more and more parents are getting behind this wonderfully old-fashioned name. With a
nifty meaning—"laughter"—Isaac is nonetheless a tad serious and scholarly, perhaps because famous bearers include
scientist Newton and violinist Stern. Ike is the more casual,

gregarious nickname. Isaac Browne Hawkins was a British poet in the eighteenth century.

Ivan: There's no way a five-year-old (or a ten-year-old) will have heard of Ivan the Terrible, so don't bypass this rich, Russian name for that reason. Ivan is a heartbeat away from Evan, and far less common. It's easy to spell and pronounce and packs a wallop of Euro-coolness in four letters. Ivan's also creeping up the list, hanging out in the 120–125 zone, so get it while the getting's good. Ivan Turgenev was one of the most admired and influential novelists of the nineteenth century with his opus *Fathers and Sons*.

Jack: Everybody loves Jack, especially screenwriters who have seriously overused it as a character name in movies and TV. Parents have followed suit, enjoying Jack's robust, happy sound: Jack's number 6 and possibly climbing upward. It may be irresistible, but do think about Mack (not even in the top 1,000), Gus, Jax, or Jed for a similar punch. Jack Kerouac was an American novelist and father of the Beat Generation who wrote *On the Road*.

Like Jack? It's number 6, so think about Mack, Gus, Jax, or Jed for a similar punch.

Jacob/Jake: Jacob means "he who supplants," and in the late nineties, Jacob displaced Michael as the number 1 boy's name in the country. (Then in 2006, Aiden unseated Jacob.) Everybody loves Jacob, and I do mean everybody, which is why it is boiling-over hot. But what's not to like, apart from utter ubiquitousness? Jacob has archaic roots in the Old Testament as the patriarch who wrestled with God and fathered the twelve tribes of Israel. Since then, Jacob has appeared in all sorts of books, from Jacob Grimm of the Brothers Grimm to Jacob Marley in *A Christmas Carol*. Because every elementary school has ten Jacobs, you have to ask yourself if you can live with such saturation. Josiah, Jonah, and Jeremiah are more atypical and also come from that great baby name sourcebook, the Good Book. Jax or Jude offer a similar confident zing and are much more inventive. By the way, you're not being creative or original if you use **Jake** instead, as so many parents have been doing. (Jake on its own is a top 60 name, as of 2006.) Jake Barnes was a character in Hemingway's *The Sun Also Rises*.

James: Here is classic baby naming at it's best: James, a name as old as the ancient Greeks and as new as the most current top 20 popularity chart. James was a book of the Bible, belonging to the author who was also the brother of Jesus. It belonged to any number of kings and noblemen,

---

Mod and Marvelous Middles

Amos ❋ Asher ❋ Basil ❋ Binx ❋ Bram ❋ Clive ❋ Darby
❋ DuBois ❋ Finn ❋ Fritz ❋ Heath ❋ Justice ❋ Keats
❋ Leo ❋ Moby ❋ Nash ❋ Paz ❋ Roark ❋ Yeats

---

as well as countless paupers and tradesmen. You won't be rocking the boat by choosing James, but you will be selecting one of the strongest and most pleasing-to-the-ear standards of all time. James Joyce and James Fenimore Cooper are just two literary idols to bear this name.

Jason: If you're consulting this book I'm doubtful you would pick Jason, but stranger things have happened, and by jingle, it's a bonafide literary (and biblical) standard. Jason is the quintessential sixties and seventies name, and likely belongs to a dozen guys or more who have made your acquaintance so far in your lifetime. In fact, chances are good that you yourself are named Jason, as most Jasons could have Jasons of their own by now. I can see the appeal: Jason sounds like a great guy who's solid and sweet. He's the kind of man who would help a pregnant woman carry her groceries to her car. Indeed, Jason was a hero of Greek mythology, leading the Argonauts in the search of the Golden Fleece.

Jasper: Cut from the same old-time-yet-newfangled cloth as Ezra, Leo, Emmett, and Phinneaus, Jasper is onward and upward. Stylish yet well built, Jasper is the name of a soap hottie too, which, trust me, is actually a good thing. Why? Because TV writers are among the most edgy, hyper-communicative people on the planet, and they've invented or resurrected heaps of goodies over time to set trends in motion. Jasper may well catch on. This was the name of a character in *The Pathfinder*, by James Fenimore Cooper, and it's also linked to artist Jasper Johns.
Nickname: Jazz

Jay: Jay Gatsby was F. Scott Fitzgerald's most enduring creation, an icon of the Jazz Age and the epicenter of one of literature's most influential novels of all time. The mysteriously rich Gatsby evokes hot jazz and cold champagne, high-maintenance women (Daisy Buchanan wrote the book on those), and a life made soft by too much too soon. It's romantic stuff (tragically romantic, if you know the book), but Jay has never really lived up to Gatsby's dapper persona. Jay's a solid forty-year-old's name, but you do hear it from time to time on a third-grader. Some other *J* names worth a look include Jasper, Jack, and Jadon (the biblical spelling only, please).

Jeremiah: Jeremiah was a bullfrog, according to Three Dog Night, but his name is surely more interesting than most others in the *J* pond. Though it flirted with the top 100, this biblical prophet's name has never been as overused as other Bible boys like Jacob and Joshua. The tanned hides and rustic aura of mountain men such as Jeremiah Johnson give this one the sound of a grizzled old coot telling stories around the campfire, which means it's perfect for today's boys. Jeremiah appears in *Swiss Family Robinson* and *Rebecca of Sunnybrook Farm*.

Johan: Coming from a German immigrant family and community, I may have passed over Johan as being too old-time "Herman the German" to fit a modern baby. (What blinders we have on toward our own culture!) But lately I've been hearing Johan as a first or middle name from people of German, Dutch, and Scandinavian lineages, and it dovetails perfectly with the ethnic tribute names out there (i.e., Anders, Lars, and Willem). Deutsch übermodel Heidi Klum and her husband, Seal, named their third child Johan. (Pronounced "Yo-hahn"; Yo is one hot little nickname.) Bach lovers might feel warmly toward this name, which was also borne by Johann Wolfgang von Goethe, the great German thinker and poet of *Faust*.

Jonah/Jonas: Jonah is a rugged, bracing name that calls up images of the wind, the sea, and, of course, large marine mammals. We named our firstborn Jonah, and I must say we have been extremely pleased in the decade since. For some bizarre reason, this *J* name never touched the Jacob and Joshua pandemic with a ten-foot pole. As an entertainment writer, I've interviewed plenty of hypercreative types who think this name stirs up themes of rejuvenation and second chances. Noah is ten times more popular, yet Jonah is the more innovative, energetic choice. From literature: Zora Neale Hurston's novel *Jonah's Gourd Vine*. (PS: Yes, our Jonah has been given lots of stuffed whales in his day, and that's a fun thing.) **Jonas** is the Greek version, and belonged to the main character of *The Giver* by Lois Lowry, which won the 1994 Newbery Medal.

Like Jacob and Joshua? Make a bigger splash with Jonah.

Jotham: Jotham ("JOH-thum") would make an exceptionally rare and vivid choice, futuristic even. This hybrid of Joshua and Ethan has a very creative sound that should appeal to independent thinkers. Jotham can hardly be found in baby-name books, never mind on the playground, so the way is clear for you to road test it on your street. That being said, it is being heard here and there in circles where Isaiah, Malachi, and Jonah are hits. But it hasn't cracked the top 1,000 yet. In the Bible, Jotham was the young, God-fearing king of Judah in the book of 2 Chronicles. He also appears as a character in *The Pioneers* by James Fenimore Cooper.

Jude: The old thinking was that Jude was too much like Judas. In fact, it was once the short form of that very name, ruined forever for obvious reasons. But Jude was a common name among biblical folk, and so untarnished that it's the name of a book of the Bible. Fast-forward to our era. Jude got a huge boost by the handsome British actor Jude Law, whose appearance in such films as *Cold Mountain* catapulted his handle from nowhere to the low 300s by 2005. On your bookshelf, Jude Hawley was the rather unhappy hero of Thomas Hardy's *Jude the Obscure*. So here's my new thinking: Not only is this a biblical name and a saint's name (Saint Jude is the patron saint of lost causes), it's literary, Beatles-esque, and beautiful. "Hey, Jude" indeed.

Julian/Julius/Jules: Gentlemanly Julian got a boost when the Jerry Seinfelds picked it as their firstborn son's name. It sounds upscale, polished, and urbane, which will appeal to some and leave others wanting more. Lately, though, Julian's been slipping in the charts in favor of more rugged dudes such as Jackson. If you like the elegance of Julian, but are uncomfortable with its closeness to Julianne, maybe Sebastian or Miles will fit the bill. Julian was one of The Famous Five, Enid Blyton's fictional group of short detectives, composed of four children (Julian, Dick, Anne, and George) and their dog Timmy. **Julius**, on the other hand, sounds a bit cooler and less ostentatious, despite having been attached to one of the most influential men in classical antiquity, Julius Caesar. The *us* ending has a robust Roman feel, plus it leaves no doubt as to the masculinity of the bearer: Julian is reading poetry on the stands while Julius is competing in shotput. Julius is a powerful leader's name, an ageless gold standard that harks back to the days when Caesar transformed the Roman Republic into the Roman Empire. Shakespeare's tragedy *Julius Caesar* details the end of his life. **Jules**, meanwhile, is the French shape of Julius, borne famously by *Twenty Thousand Leagues Under the Sea* scribe Jules Verne. This is definitely a female-sounding name on this side of the Atlantic, thanks in part to entertainment journalist Jules Asner.

> Julian is reading poetry on the stands while Julius is competing in shotput.

Jupiter: If this universe is too constraining, step into the fifth dimension with Jupiter, a wildly iconoclastic name that may make some people think you've been visiting the planetarium too often. Here's the thing: Those who matter will get used to it, as people are wont to do with any singular name. Others just don't matter. What may be significant, though, is the phenomenal namesake, Jupiter Hammond, the founder of African American literature. A slave, Hammond was the first black person in the United

> Jupiter Hammond was the founder of African American literature.

States to be published when his poem appeared in 1760, and his "Address to the Negroes of the State of New York" speech still inspires and rouses readers.

Justice: No one bats an eye over Grace, Hope, and Faith, but somehow virtue names have never been as popular for boys. Justice, though, could be an exception, a grand and gorgeous-sounding name that is a mere heartbeat away from the trendoid Justin, but more compelling. Talk about a strong name that conveys potency, integrity, and truth— Justice rocks. If you want to back down a little bit from the in-your-face word *Justice*, the spelling **Justus** works too. Along with True and Noble, Justice makes a magnetic middle name with loads of character. Justice was a minor character in Shakespeare's *Measure for Measure*.

Keats: It's no wonder Keats means "kite": it's breezy, sunshiny, and full of verve. Yes, you'd be naming your son after one of the core poets of the English Romantic period, but somehow Keats sounds like a happy-go-lucky guy playing Frisbee with his dog. Like Yeats, this one could work fantastically well as a sharp middle name too.

Kenneth: It's quite premature for this old Scottish name to ripen again, what with the last blast of status being as early as the 1970s. We all know more than one Ken (who may well be hitched to Barbie), and since it rocked the baby name charts of the forties and fifties, he could be your dad or father-in-law. Give it another generation, when we are all grandparents, and it may sound exciting and novel to our babies as they pore over books like this one. At any rate, Kenneth was a character in Sir Walter Scott's *The Talisman*. Kenneth Grahame wrote *The Wind in the Willows*.

Kingsley: Kingsley might sound a little too uppity for most, but in the wake of rock baby Kingston Rossdale (Gwen Stefani and Gavin Rossdale's boy), it's more in the realm of possibility. King is the obvious short form, but I've also heard Kin. I must say that Kingston, though not technically a lit name like Kingsley, hits both the surname and place name hot spots, and its countless mentions in the media affords it accessibility. But getting back to the name at hand. Sir Kingsley William Amis was an English novelist, poet, critic, and teacher. He wrote more than twenty novels, including *Lucky Jim*.

   Nickname: King

Langston: You might think Langston is solely the province of African Americans, proud of the Harlem Renaissance poet Hughes who portrayed the black middle class with lives full of struggle, joy, laughter, and music. "Night is beautiful," he wrote in his poem "My People," "So the faces of my people." This handsome, completely untrendy name (not even a scratch on the top 1,000 yet!) is definitely a fabulous pick for those proud of their black identity; it's also perfect for anyone looking to evoke the Renaissance or the hip, history-making blues clubs in which Hughes would jot down poems as he soaked in the music of the twenties and thirties. Langston dovetails with your Peytons and Kingstons and has a slick short form, Lang. This all leads me to believe that it's a prehot name. Incidentally, Langston was named after his mother's maiden name. He was born James Mercer Langston Hughes.

Nickname: Lang

Lear: "All that glitters," said King Lear, "is not gold." He could have been talking about some of the shiny, faddish names that are going around these days. Lear wouldn't be one of them, though like the jet, it's sleek and aerodynamic. Shakespeare's *King Lear* was based on the legendary **Leir** of Britain, who really did have three daughters, knights, a castle, and the whole nine yards. Both spellings would mesh well with punchy, nickname-proof hits such as Luke, Jack, and Max, but Lear has more panache and originality.

Lennox: Does this name just crackle with energy or what? Maybe it's the strong link to muscle-bound boxer Lennox Lewis, or the similarity to high-profile rising star Maddox, or that extraordinary *x* finale. Whatever the cause, Lennox's commanding clout cannot be ignored. It also fits in with the surname rage as a blue-blooded Scotch option. (There's a Duke of Lennox and an Earl of Lennox—heck, even Annie Lennox is Scottish!) In Shakespeare's *The Merchant of Venice*, Lennox is—what else?—a Scottish nobleman.

Leo: This hot little hipster sounds so of the moment, it's hard to believe the lit namesake, Leo Tolstoy, died about a hundred years ago. The *o* finale of these three letters adds instant energy and punch, and, hey, any link with Leonardo DiCaprio is a good thing. But back to Tolstoy: He was a Russian novelist and philosopher whose peace-loving views influenced Gandhi and Martin Luther King Jr. He wrote *Anna Karenina* and, of course, that tome of tomes, *War and Peace* (which we've all been meaning to get to, haven't we?).

This hot little hipster sounds so of the moment, it's hard to believe the lit namesake, Leo Tolstoy, died about a hundred years ago.

Leon: Since Paul Reiser named his first son Ezra (which actually provided the initial spark in us doing the same), I was avidly curious to find out what Reiser would choose for another boy. Turns out he chose Leon, which I never would have guessed in a million years. So, Leon: a boxer, a jazz and blues great in a panama hat (as in Leon "Salty" Redbone). Stick it on a little suburban kid and it kind of cracks me up. With all of those hepcat references, Leon does indeed sound smooth and ultrahip. Call it "prefashionable," and watch for Leon to possibly ride Leo's coattails. The Europeans are digging it already. Leon DuPuis, by the way, was a major character in Flaubert's *Madame Bovary*.

Lewis: Little Lewis would make a great sibling for Henry, Charlie, Katherine, or Emmaline. Lewis is like a solemn Beefeater with a twinkle in his eye: he's gentlemanly with a splash of mischief. Lew or Lou are relaxed, cozy, and sound about as cool as Gus, Max, and Harry. Lewis Carroll authored *Alice's Adventures in Wonderland*, but your

Lewis may tap into C. S. Lewis, author of the Narnia books, as a more manly affiliate. It's strong and gentle at the same time.

Nicknames: Lou, Lew

Lincoln: Lincoln is pretty much the perfect name: uncommon, cool, and with a creative kick. It also has the homey, Honest Abe thing going for it, and the mod nickname Linc. Fellow presidential name Jackson is ten times more popular, while similar sounding Landon and Logan are top 30 hotties. Where am I going with this? Lincoln is your saving grace from generic baby naming. Snag it and run for the hills (or the hospital). Caveat: Watch your last name, because if it's Ford, you have a car dealership, not a name. Lincoln appeared in Shakespeare's *Henry IV*.

Linus: So the guy was attached to his blankie—is that such a crime? Yes, it's the fundamental Linus of *Peanuts* fame of whom I speak, and yes, parents shy away from the name because of its Charlie Brown connection. This sort of baffles me, because it's not a bad affiliation by any means. Though people will think instantly of Lucy's little brother, don't forget about these other famous Linuses: there's the mythological Linus, son of Apollo, as well as the Linus

---

Euro-Coolest

Anton ❊ August ❊ Hugo ❊ Lorenzo ❊ Lucan ❊ Magnus
❊ Manolo ❊ Nils ❊ Orlando ❊ Otto ❊ Sebastian

---

played by Humphrey Bogart in the old movie *Sabrina*, starring Audrey Hepburn as the woman he loves. One theater couple I know dubbed their fourth child Linus, which fits perfectly—it says to all the watching world, "You can keep your Austins and your Ethans, we're going out on a long limb here." It's creative, cute, and has no chance whatsoever of cracking the top 1,000 in this lifetime.

London: London could be the new Paris, although here's hoping another bubbleheaded heiress won't emerge to ruin the name for both sexes. Right now, it's sophisticated without being stuffy, and gently evocative of Trafalgar Square and the Thames. London has a global vibe to it, as all great place-names do, but it hasn't been overused yet. Be aware, though, that it's quietly moving upwards for girls and boys. As a lit name, this was Jack London's surname. It's also considered a "character" in all of Charles Dickens's works because he vividly drew every quarter of the city he knew so well.

Lorenzo: Say this name out loud a few times and see if you don't get a little light-headed. (In fact, it might be worth naming your child this just so you can say it out loud seventy-five million times.) Keep the smelling salts handy, and if you have any claim whatsoever on an Italian or Spanish heritage, please pick Shakespearean Lorenzo, I beg you. It has the vibe of a guy with smoldering eyes who plays Spanish guitar, rescues people from burning buildings, and also finds time to compete in triathlons. I think he may also make paella. And Enzo? Now that's snazzy.

Nickname: Enzo

Lucan: If you love the sound of Luke (a top 30 name) and Lucas (a top 50) but don't like their high rankings, have I got a deal for you: Lucan. It sounds made-up, but this archaic Roman name is anything but. Instead, the noble appellation has been around since at least 39 AD, when the poet Marcus Annaeus Lucanus, known as Lucan, was born. (That guy was regarded as one of the stellar figures of the Silver Latin period of epic poetry.) This old Roman name somehow became Irish (bonus points), and is still today. Another literary reference: Sir Lucan is one of the Knights of the Round Table in the Arthurian legend. Handsome and warriorlike, Lucan is completely yours for the taking.

Lucius: Lucius is luscious, but don't pronounce it that way (it's "LOO-shus"). A name as old as the Roman coliseums, Lucius belonged to popes and saints and was one of the Bard's favorites. He used Lucius as a character name in *Julius Caesar*, *Titus Andronicus*, and *Timon of Athens*. The only "issue," if you can call it that, is the rather malevolent presence of Lucius Malfoy in the Harry Potter books. Lucius does have a darkish, brooding air, but that can also be interpreted as mysterious and exotic.

Maddox: Baby-naming force of nature Angelina Jolie can take all the credit for single-handedly unearthing this fantastic Welsh last name and applying it to her adorable Cambodian son. (Vietnamese Pax is her second son, which makes me tempted to send her thank-you notes for the grand-scale *x* resurgence in baby naming.) Groovy global Maddox is burly and tough yet sleek and handsome too. (See Lennox for another hip *x* ending.) Ford Madox Ford wrote *The Good Soldier*.

Nickname: Mad

Magnus: Magnus has inherent grandeur because it means "the great one"; plus, it was used by Scandinavian kings. Its majesty is nicely offset by a cozy and quirky quality that keeps it from taking itself too seriously, attributes possibly taken into consideration by actor and funnyman Will Ferrell when he chose this for his son. Bonus: if you're Scandinavian or Scottish, this is an ethnic favorite. Magnus Eisengrim is one of the major characters in the Deptford Trilogy books, written by Robertson Davies.

Malachi: Kill three birds with one stone by appropriating the biblical, literary, and Celtic favorite Malachi. (In Ireland, Malachy, pronounced "MA-la-kee," is well used as a saint's name.) On a quest for a snappy Bible name that will leave Mark and Matthew in the dust? Malachi was the last of the twelve minor prophets and had his own book of the Bible. Literary peg: Malachi Malagrowther was the pseudonym used for Sir Walter Scott and a character name in the Irish novels of James Joyce. More and more parents in North America are choosing this fresher-than-the-usual-biblical-suspects name.

> Kill three birds with one stone by appropriating the biblical, literary, and Celtic favorite Malachi.

Nicknames: Mac, Mal, and Chi ("Kai")

Malcolm: This doesn't say "I eat haggis" as much as Angus, Fergus, and Lorcan, et al., but Malcolm still has a quietly plaid vibe that's manly and appealing. Of course, there was nothing quiet about Malcolm X, and his many namesakes were so dubbed because of his activist zeal. If you combine the Scottish charm with the passionate fervor of X, you have a handsome, underused name you can be proud of, no matter your ethnic background. Malcolm was a character in *Macbeth*.

Manolo: The perfect name for the son of a shoe over-achiever! Manolo is kind of swanky sounding, even if you take that crazy-spendy Manolo Blahnik footwear out of the equation. This variation of Manuel has a serious Latin flair. In *Shadow of a Bull*, the 1965 Newbery Medal–winning novel by Maia Wojciechowska, a young Spanish boy named Manolo Oliver trains to be a matador like his fabled dead father.

Marcus/Marco: Marcus is one of the oldest names around, having been minted as early as the second century, when it belonged to every tenth boy on the block (including a future Roman emperor). In North America, it's hovered near or in the top 100 for decades. Emperor Marcus Aurelius's work *Meditations*, written on campaign between 170 and 180, is still revered and quoted as a literary monument to a government of service and duty. **Marco** adds infinite zest to Mark, and is less used than Marcus. With that Italian charisma and an *o* at the end, Marco is a head-turner. Jill Hennessy used this for her son. Marco is a character in Arthur Miller's play *A View from the Bridge*.

Max/Maxim: If you're going to maximize Max (the yummy little imp in Maurice Sendak's *Where the Wild Things Are*), think about choosing the Russian gent Maxim. It's chicer and more global than Maxwell, and really, what does it matter anyway? You're going to call the boy Max from day one. I have yet to meet a Maxwell or Maximus or Maximilian who goes by anything but the first three letters. Maxim Gorky was a Soviet/Russian author, a founder of the socialist realism literary method and a political activist.

Miguel: Miguel is Michael florescent. Even though it is merely the Spanish translation of the everyguy name of the century, Miguel brings tons of Latin charm, flourish, and color to the table. It's a gorgeous choice, especially for those who have some attachment to a Hispanic culture (i.e., your husband's grandmother was Mexican) but haven't grown up in it. Don Miguel de Cervantes y Saavedra was a Spanish novelist, poet, and playwright. His novel *Don Quixote* is considered a founding classic of Western literature. He has been dubbed el Príncipe de los Ingenios ("the Prince of Wits").

Miles: With a historically verifiable pilgrim backbone (Miles Standish was on the *Mayflower*) and the jazzy vibe added by Miles Davis, this one's smooth and classical but a bit of a hipster, too. In literature, Miles Hendon was a character in Mark Twain's *The Prince and the Pauper*, while the historical guy figured prominently in Longfellow's poem "The Courtship of Miles Standish."

Miller: When ultrachic fashion designer (and Beatles child) Stella McCartney named her son Miller, she turned some heads with her pioneering pick. She was the first, but not the last, high-profile parent to appropriate this erstwhile tradesman handle as a style-making ID. Miller has a lot going for it, including a smooth and masculine sound, a hip vibe, and not one but two trends—surnames and tradesman names. While today's little Miller might not do much grain grinding, his name still carries a vestige of good old-fashioned, work-with-your-hands honor. It's a winner to watch. Arthur Miller was one of the greatest playwrights of the twentieth century. His works include *The Crucible* and *Death of a Salesman*.

Milo: The first Aerosmith grandchild had to have a smokin'-cool name, and sure enough, Liv Tyler and her own rocker husband presented Grandpa Steven with Milo. That *o* ending just rocks, speaking of the genre, and the whole thing is fun, dashing, cute, and arty in one easy-to-spell, approachable package. Milo could be a skateboarder, a poet, a lacrosse player, a drummer, or all of the above. The appeal is huge. I have no doubt whatsoever that this name will rise—it might start off slowly at first, because it takes some getting used to, but it will take off in its own sweet time. Milo was a character in *Catch-22*.

Old Coot: New Cool

(i.e.: Used to sound like a grandpa name, but now sounds superhip on a baby. Go figure!)

Amos ❋ Barnaby ❋ Chester ❋ Ezra ❋ Gus ❋ Homer
❋ Jasper ❋ Silas ❋ Truman ❋ Whitman

Mitchell: Here's a tougher-sounding surname than Logan, Jackson, or Carson, but it would go well with all those (much) trendier names. The short form Mitch retains its cool jock vibe while still maintaining a softer side. Bonus: this is one of those "Oh yeah! We could have named our baby [fill in the blank]" names that everyone likes, but is off the radar nowadays. Margaret Mitchell was the Pulitzer Prize–winning author of *Gone With the Wind*, which has sold more hardcover copies of any book apart from the Bible.

Nickname: Mitch

Moby: It's short, punchy, and very quirky, but Moby could easily work as a first name. A heartbeat away from Toby, Moby is—wait for it—a whale of a name. The techno music performer Moby (born Richard Melville Hall) took his nickname from the novel *Moby-Dick*, which was written by Herman Melville, his great-great-granduncle.

Moby (born Richard Melville Hall) took his nickname from the novel *Moby-Dick*, which was written by Herman Melville, his great-great-granduncle.

Morrison: Morris may sound like a fuddy-duddy, but what about Morrison? To me, it sounds light-years cooler, probably because the immediate evocation is of the Doors and their cute, floppy-haired lead singer singing, "C'mon, baby, light my fire." Jim Morrison wrote poetry, and Toni Morrison won the Pulitzer Prize for *Beloved* and the Nobel Prize in 1993 for her collected works. Check out Moe as a good-humored short form.

Nicknames: Morris, Moe

Moses: It seems like just yesterday that Moses would be considered way too much for a little tyke to bear. Under the Cecil B. DeMille regime, when the name was burdened with images of Charleton Heston's snowy beard and epic hairdo, Moses sounded altogether too ponderous. Today Moe's got a new MO: Coldplay Baby, not to mention the amazing *Prince of Egypt*. That animated film definitely injected some youthful vitality to the name, making it a plausible if not completely accessible choice. With Gwyneth Paltrow and Chris Martin naming their son Moses (Apple was a hard act to follow), there's no telling where this biblical relic will go next. The name is already on the upswing, and I can see why. It—and its nickname Moe—are uncommonly cool.

Nickname: Moe

Mulligan: This old-fashioned, jauntily Irish surname comes with a fabulous children's classic: *Mike Mulligan and His Steam Shovel*, the beloved 1939 chestnut by Virginia Lee Burton about a steam shovel operator facing competition from modern, diesel-powered shovels. I think it's absolutely charming, with a boisterous personality and a cheery sound. Mully could work as a nickname, too, à la Sully and Sullivan.

Nickname: Mully

Munro: Like Murphy, Miller, and Finlay, Munro is a jazzy, compact surname that wins extra points for its friendliness, tartan vibe, and presidential underpinnings. Plus, there's the matter of that always-hip *o* ending, which always kicks up a name nicely. There was a character named Monroe Stahr who was a famous producer in *The Love of the Last Tycoon* by F. Scott Fitzgerald, but the main lit hero is Alice

Munro, the award-winning Canadian short-story writer and novelist who is widely considered one of the world's premier fiction writers. Her latest work, as of 2006, is *The View from Castle Rock*.

Nash: Cash would make a fabulous music tribute name and Dash is a rising star and celebrity pick.... How about Nash? It has the easygoing, country feel of Cash, and it's as dashing as Dash. (There you are: an accidental poem!) Nash is already a hottie on daytime television, which, even if you never tune in, means promising things. It's also a lit tribute, paying homage to the irreverent punster and poet Ogden Nash who was honored in 2002 by the U.S. Postal Service with a stamp featuring his mug and six poems.

Nathaniel: With bookish good looks, not to mention a biblical pedigree as one of Jesus' disciples (spelled Nathanael), this one's a winner on many levels. Nathaniel is dignified without being boring, and he's handsome, old-fashioned, and friendly. Nathaniel Hawthorne was the great Romantic writer who penned such stalwarts as *The Scarlet Letter* and *The House of the Seven Gables*. If you're worried about this appellation being too long, Nate is a tried-and-true nickname, and Nat adds some of Nat King Cole's jazzy charm.

Ned: This quaint, dashing miniature of Edward could easily be used from cradle to grave all on its own. Ned is short, nickname-proof (because it's already a nickname), and packs a nice style punch. In books, Ned is exceptionally well represented. Ned Nickerson is Nancy Drew's long-suffering boyfriend, introduced in *The Clue in the Diary* and then appearing in nearly every story, patiently supporting gal pal Nancy in her sleuthing exploits. Another high-profile character is Ned Land, the Canadian master harpooner who accompanies Captain Nemo and others on the submarine *Nautilus* as they fight sea monsters and gather scientific evidence in *Twenty Thousand Leagues Under the Sea*.

Nemo: No, no, not the little orange fish from the 'toon. I'm referring here to the multiple Nemos in literature. There's a Nemo in Shakespeare, one in Jules Verne's *Twenty Thousand Leagues Under the Sea* and *Mysterious Island* (that would be Captain Nemo), and one in Dickens's *Bleak House*. Such a literary pedigree! And yet, we must get back to the fish, who will forever affiliate your child with the animated Nemo. If you can handle that, Nemo is one hot little name.

Nicholas/Niccolo: Nicholas conveys character, nobility, charm, and sweetness in one fell swoop—qualities that have entrenched it in the top 10 for a decade or more. This means like-minded parents who admire its history and handsomeness have pretty much found it irresistible. In fact, it's so irre-

---

Top 10 Bible Boys

Abram ❊ Amos ❊ Asher ❊ Ezra ❊ Gideon ❊ Jonah ❊ Jude ❊ Malachi ❊ Moses ❊ Silas

---

sistible that it's now reached a state of critical mass. If you cannot stay away—and I admit that Nick is a fabulous thing for a boy to be called—won't you at least consider a variation from your own ethnic background? Nicolaas (Dutch), Nikolaus (German), Niccolo (Italian; **Niccolo** Machiavelli wrote *The Prince*), Nikolai (Russian; see below), Nico (Spanish), and Nils (Scandanavian; see below). *Nicholas Nickleby* is one of Dickens's best-loved tales.

Nikolai: Nicholas is one of the top names (number 8) out there, because everyone loves that gorgeous, manly sound and connection with Saint Nick. How about getting sneaky and using one of Nick's ethnic forms to jazz it up a little? Russian-infused Nikolai, in addition to being a great hockey name (Nikolai Khabibulin, etc.), was also a character in Turgenev's great work *Fathers and Sons*.

Nils: In an era where we all seem to want to pay homage to our forbears, "immigrant" names such as Nils sound like tribute music to our ears. A Norwegian form of Nicholas, Nils is a neat little name that makes a towheaded youngster seem even blonder and adds a cool kicker from the Old Country. If your old country happens to be Sweden or Norway, grab this winning name while other Scandi-hoovians are still mulling over Lars and Anders. Nils Krogstad is a character in Ibsen's play *A Doll's House*, and *The Wonderful Adventures of Nils* is a Swedish standard published a century ago by Selma Lagerlof.

Noah: How'd that happen? Noah is in the top 10! (Wasn't he just building his ark, like, three thousand years ago?)

x

Well, it is hard to think of a name that immediately evokes kindness, strength of character, handsomeness, and old-fashioned, rugged appeal, all rolled into one. It's a fabulous, beautiful, hot name, but that's the problem: it's just too hot. If you're looking for something less overdone, consider Jonah, Micah, or Eli, straightforward, Old Testament stalwarts with all of Noah's considerable charm. In Dickens's *Oliver Twist*, Noah Claypole is the undertaker Sowerberry's apprentice, and Noah Webster is the dictionary maven.

Noah float your boat? Consider Jonah, Micah, or Eli for something more novel from the Good Book.

Obadiah: Back in Old Testament days, Obadiah was like the Tyler of the Israelites—the name was so popular that it was given to no fewer than twelve men in Scripture, including a prince and the most famous name-model, the prophet and author of the Book of Obadiah. Fast-forward a few millennia, and Obadiah sounds a bit white-bearded, robed, and sandaled. But wait, didn't Josiah, Moses, and Jeremiah sound that way until, like, five minutes ago? If you think you can pull it off, Obadiah is the slam dunk king of grizzled old coots, which means it could sound incredibly hip and vibrant on a little boy. Plus, how cute is adorable Obie, which was surprisingly well used all on its own in the first part of the last century. As long as your last name isn't Wan

Kenobi, you're in good shape. Obadiah Slope was a character in *Barchester Towers* by Anthony Trollope.

Nicknames: O, Obie

O'Casey/O'Neill: Beige Neal gets a splash of color by adding a big, beautiful O at the beginning. O'Kelly and O'Keefe have some traction out in the real world; why not honor a beloved Neal or Neil by following suit? Eugene O'Neill was the multi-Pulitzer and Nobel Prize–winning playwright of *The Iceman Cometh* and *Long Day's Journey into Night*, which is considered his masterwork. As we continue to play with the O prefix, let's look at **O'Casey** as an option. By adding the O, Casey is made even smilier, friendlier, and more Irish than before. Seán O'Casey, born in 1880, was a major Irish dramatist and the first playwright of note to write about the Dublin working classes in such works as *Juno and the Paycock* and *The Plough and the Stars*.

Nickname: O

Oliver: Victorian revival Oliver is cuddly, loveable, and just a tiny bit quirky, which should endear it to parents on a quest for something offbeat but not *too* out there. This goes perfectly with other newly dusted gems such as Violet, Lucy, or Phoebe, or with trendy favorites such as Jackson or Hayden. Remember, that O initial is a prized one, and beyond Owen and Otis, it's pretty slim pickings. *Oliver Twist* is one of Charles Dickens's most beloved fictional creations.

Nickname: Ollie

Omar: A name that is truly multicultural in its appeal to African American, Latino, Arabic people, and other ethnic tribes, Omar is a mysterious package in recognizable wrapping. Omar also begins with that punchy letter O, which makes it that much more appealing and strong. Omar Khayyam was the Persian poet who died in 1131 and left behind a long legacy of his scientific accomplishments and his best-known poem, "The Rubáiyát of Omar Khayyám." He's been quoted widely, including in Martin Luther King Jr.'s speech "Why I Oppose the War in Vietnam."

Orion: "It's kind of like Ryan with an O," you might begin your goodwill campaign with the relatives. Indeed, this is one cosmic customer who sounds surprisingly familiar to almost everyone, between Ryan and the well-known constellation. Orion would be an exceptionally virile, creative, and muscular choice, with a fun pinch of sci-fi. You and your son will love connecting the stars of his "namesake" constellation together on clear nights. In Greek mythology, Orion was a colossal hunter.

Orlando: This name practically makes me swoon just saying it out loud, such is its swashbuckling, romantic aura. (Okay, so the "swashbuckling" I get from Orlando Bloom's portrayal of a hottie pirate in *Pirates of the Caribbean*.) But there's a deeper romantic history there: Orlando falls in love at first sight with Rosalind in *As You Like It*. Later, having been banished

> With Orlando, you can't really go more suave short of Romeo or Don Juan.

to the forest, he writes simple love poems to her on trees. You can't really go more suave here short of Romeo or Don Juan. This one will make the girls melt. Perhaps Orlando Bloom will do for his debonair name what Leonardo DiCaprio did for his.

Orsino: An O at the beginning and an *o* at the end? What could be yummier? Indeed, this Italian form of Orson is delicious, spicy, and makes one crave pasta in the worst way. People are really grooving on O names these days: Owen and Olivia are smash hits and Otis and Oliver are gathering steam. Orsino is the wilder option, but with those O bookends, it might be worth it. The Orsino of *Twelfth Night*, the Bard's male lead in his popular comedy, was most likely based on Orsini, Duke of Bracciano, an Italian nobleman who visited London in the winter of 1600.

Oscar: Here's a hipster that came from the same cigar-smoking, deli-frequenting grandpa resuscitation as Sam, Harry, Max, and Leo. The picky guy in your life probably will shoot this down fast: "Oscar the Grouch?" But c'mon, he is kind of cute in a green, shaggy, curmudgeonly kind of way! Anyway, who cares? This name has loads of edgy, vintage charm and it sounds just perfect for parents who want something more fascinating and gritty than the usual suspects. O is a stupendous first letter, and Oscar's more vibrant and colorful (no, not green) than cuddly Owen. Oscar Wilde was the Irish playwright and poet who wrote *The Importance of Being Earnest* and *An Ideal Husband*. A more modern affiliation is Oscar Hijuelos, the Cuban American writer of the Pulitzer Prize–winning *The Mambo Kings Plays Songs of Love*.

Otto: Up until very recently, this name seemed quite fusty, lederhosened, and hopelessly outmoded. Then one day some avant-garde parents flipped it around, turning fusty into quirky, lederhosened into Euro-cool, and outmoded into unearthed treasure. Plus, that bouncy O initial is in somewhat short supply beyond Owen and Otis. *Achtung* Otto! It starts and ends with an O! It's the same backward and forward! Everyday is Octoberfest with Otto! Clearly, I've become carried away, but seriously, folks, how funky can you get? And, psst…no one is really using this hep-cat—yet. Otto was a character in *Journey to the Center of the Earth*, a classic 1864 science fiction novel by Jules Verne.

Ovid: Okay, kids, buckle your seat belts—you're in for a bumpy ride if you choose this humdinger. The relatives will become agitated, and there's not much you can say to calm them down. If the family isn't a concern of yours, then perhaps drastic departures from the status quo are more of a priority. Ovid veers way off the beaten path of the last two millennia. At least you won't be going so far as Ovid's parents, who in 43 BC dubbed their baby Publius Ovidius Naso. When Ovid grew up, he wrote epic poems—including perhaps his best-known work, *Metamorphoses*—that ranked right up there with Homer and Virgil. If you name your child Ovid, you should get a medal for bravery, and you also have my hearty congratulations.

Owen: You've got to watch the wily Welsh. They come at you subtly with names like Jennifer or Dylan, which at first sound wildly original and cool. Then one day you wake up, and every third person in the third grade has that name. The same thing has happened with Owen, an adorable, strong, and Celtic-flavored option that ends in *en*—it's the perfect thing to call your boy! But when you peek at the chart, you realize that Owen is now a top 40 commodity. Oscar, Otis, and Oliver are fresher O boys at this point. I know, *I know.* You still love

Like Owen? Consider Oscar, Otis, and Oliver.

it. Well, I don't blame you, because it's fabulous. Blame it on the Welsh, and remember: they're stealthy. (Owen Glendowner was in the Bard's *Henry IV, Part 2.*)

Pablo: This is a rebellious and radical choice if you don't have Spanish ethnicity. (If you're looking for an example of non-Latin Latin naming, there's Frances McDormand and Ethan Cohen, who named their son Pedro.) Pablo is light, but it's leavened by the intense namesake Pablo Neruda, the controversial and much-loved Chilean poet who was awarded the Nobel Prize for literature at the end of his life. References to his poetry are sprinkled throughout literature and pop culture, in everything from a *Simpsons* episode to the musical *Rent*. The year he died, Neruda's house was searched by soldiers from a military dictatorship. He famously said, "Look around—there's only one thing of danger for you here—poetry." If you too think poetry is dangerous, Pablo might be a fitting choice.

Paz: In turbulent times, a name full of concord and reconciliation is meaningful. Paz means "peace" in Spanish, and, like Latin brother Pax (chosen by turbo baby namer Angelina Jolie for her fourth child), it suggests harmony, justice, and the harder work that peace entails. If you don't want to go as far as using it as a first name (we can't all be as brave as Angelina), Paz is perfect as a middle moniker: short, sweet, and succinctly political. Octavio Paz was the Mexican Nobel Prize–winning essayist who delved into politics, economics, and Aztec art among his topics. He is best known for his book-length essay, *El laberinto de la soledad* (*The Labyrinth of Solitude*).

Peter: In a world of Jaydens, Kylers, and Gages, Peter sounds most untrendy. For some of you, that's the appeal. Peter is biblical—he was one of the most high-profile disciples—ancient, and also old-fashioned in a turn-of-the-century way. You won't rock the boat by choosing Peter, and that's exactly what you may want: safe, solid, and salt of the earth. Peters have populated pumpkin patches and books for eons: Peter Pan and Peter Cottontail both come to mind as kid-friendly connections. Plus, not every name

---

Lorilee's Top 20 Boys' Names

Amos ❖ Atticus ❖ Cormac ❖ Ezra ❖ Dashiell ❖ Finn
❖ Gus ❖ Jasper ❖ Jonah ❖ Jude ❖ Lennox
❖ Leo ❖ Lucan ❖ Moses ❖ Oliver ❖ Otto ❖ Sawyer
❖ Sebastian ❖ Silas ❖ Truman

---

has "the Great" attached to it by way of history. If you're not brushed up on your Russian history, Peter the Great ruled Russia for forty-three years in the 1700s.

Nickname: Pete, Petie

Philemon: If you want to take old-fashioned charm to the nth degree, check out Philemon, an ancient Greek name that just might float in this topsy-turvy era where fuddy-duddies such as Phineus, Josiah, and Gideon sound hip. Philemon's yet another old coot that could be turned upside down and given fresh life on a little boy. And Phi is one hepcat nickname, you must admit. In the Bible, the book of Philemon is just twenty-five verses in length, and was written by Paul to his friend, the affluent Colossian Philemon. This name also appears in Shakespeare's *Pericles*.

Nickname: Phi

Philip/Pip: Though Philip has an illustrious history as a name, the Greek alias ("lover of horses") still suffers from some PR issues: belonging to lots of kings and a current Prince, Philip is probably always going to sound upper-crust. In the Bible, Philip was an apostle, which paved the way for sainthood and caused countless people to use the designation over the last couple of millenniums. It's peppered all over classic literature, including Shakespeare. One quirkier reference is Philip Marlowe, the cool detective character in Raymond Chandler's 1930s novels, including *The Big Sleep*. **Pip** was the nickname for Philip, Dickens's core character in *Great Expectations*.

Nicknames: Phil, Pip, Flip

Philo: Pronounced "FY-lo" (not "PHIL-o"), this is a very hip, almost unheard-of name that could catch on in the wake of Milo's budding popularity. This philosophical name belonged to a great number of ancient thinkers, and it has the best meaning: "love of" or "loving." This would suit a truly iconoclastic family on a quest for something unusual yet not too weird. If you want to lengthen it, Philostrate is the master of revels at Theseus's court in Shakespeare's *A Midsummer Night's Dream*.

Phineas: You can always count on celebrities to blaze new baby name trails. And why not? They just don't care as much as the rest of us what people will think of their child's name, so they go for it. Case in point: Julia Roberts's Phinneaus, twin brother to Hazel, known as Finn. This is reverse cool at its finest, like those white loafers some men are wearing: at first they shock you with their audacity and so-far-out-they're-in derring-do, but then you kind of admire the wearers for their chutzpah. Phineas also belonged to several literary characters, including one in *The Pallisers* by Trollope and, more currently, to Phineas, known as Finny, in John Knowles's prep school classic *A Separate Peace*. Take a cue from Julia and Knowles and use Finn or Finny as slick short forms.

Nicknames: Phin, Finn, Finney

Pierre: Here's another example of a common cultural name (it's the French form of Peter) that would be perfect for someone who wants to keep a fading element of their ethnicity alive for the next generation. (See also Miguel, Nils, and Johan.) In France and Quebec, of course, Pierre is akin to Michael or David or Peter—an ordinary Joe Schmoe name. But on a child with, say, a French great-grandfather, Pierre reawakens a dying branch of the family tree. Plus, everyone's heard the name Pierre, so no one will be freaked out that it's too Gallic, like Aurelien or Didier. Pierre is smooth and sophisticated while still being perfectly approachable. In literature, Pierre looms large as the marine biologist narrator Aronnax of *Twenty Thousand Leagues Under the Sea* and the central character Bezukhov of *War and Peace*.

Piers: Here's a novel way to honor a family member named Peter while adding quite a bit more dash and style. This sounds a lot like steely Pierce (in fact, Pierce means "son of Piers"), but it's slightly softer. It could be the middle English form of Peter—think the humble plough-

> Piers is a novel way to honor a family member named Peter while adding more dash and style.

man of *Piers Plowman*, which was written by William Langland in the fourteenth century and ranks up there with Chaucer's *Canterbury Tales* as one of the early great works of English literature.

Poe/Pod: Poe might be up for consideration as a first name if there wasn't the matter of the red Teletubbie, but it is what it is. As a middle name, though, Poe is arty and spare and could be used for a boy or a girl. (You might want to wait a few years, though, before reading "The Fall of the House of Usher" as a bedtime story.) Edgar Allan Poe's black humor and tales of the macabre influenced lots of creepy, twisted tales. As for **Pod**, only committed iconoclasts need apply. Pod Clock was one of the Borrowers (from the series by Mary Norton). Pod is described as having a "round, currant-bunny sort of face." Sounds like a baby to me.

Porthos: Let's say you have boy triplets. Wouldn't it be neato to have them chanting, "One for all and all for one," like Porthos, Athos, and Aramis, the Three Musketeers? Alexandre Dumas would be so pleased. It was he who concocted the inseparable musketeers and their friend D'Artagnan in 1844. Not having triplets? Oh well. It was just a thought.

 Q

Quebec: Looking for a Q name that you can also visit on vacation? No? Well, let's talk about the possibilities of Quebec anyway, in case you change your mind. This beautiful French-speaking province and city in Canada makes for a cool place-name along the lines of Adelaide, Brooklyn, and Savannah. Need a precedence? Quebec is a very minor character in Dickens's *Bleak House*. The nickname options here are quite hip: Q and Bec.

   Nicknames: Q, Bec

Quentin: If you are drawn to the ever-popular two-syllable names ending in the *en* sound—Aiden, Logan, or Landon—happy, hunky Quentin could be your saving grace from choosing something that's overused. That first letter Q not only infuses the name with a dash of creative quirkiness, it also serves as a built-in nickname with loads of snap, crackle, and pop. Quentin Compson is a main character in William Faulkner's masterpiece *The Sound and the Fury*.

Nicknames: Q, Quent

Quintus: This name is so resonant of coliseums and gladiators, it sounds a bit like an archeological find from some Roman ruin. The ancient Eternal City had a top 20 and only a top 20, and Quintus was on it (along with pals Marcus, Brutus, and Titus). Quintus is an old-new spin on Quentin with a surprise ending and the nifty feel of a relic. But...I'm not finished yet! Along with every selection of the name Quintus, you also get, at no additional charge, the sharp-every-time nickname Quin. Quintus was Titus's son in Shakespeare's *Titus Andronicus*.

> Along with every selection of the name Quintus, you also get, at no additional charge, the sharp-every-time nickname Quin.

Nicknames: Q, Quin, Quint

R

Remus: Ready for adventures in baby naming? Parents on the prowl for something truly unshackled and singular have a gutsy choice in Remus. It's strikingly handsome, with a strong Roman profile and significant ties to literature. In ancient times, Remus and his brother Romulus were known as the traditional founders of Rome, appearing in mythology as the twin sons of Rhea and Mars. Then in 1881, Joel

Chandler Harris wrote *Uncle Remus*, whose title character was also the fictional narrator for a collection of African American folktales. And finally, Remus John Lupin is a character in the Harry Potter books. It's a triple literary threat.

> **R**emus is a triple literary threat.

Rhett: Suave, dashing Rhett will always have the rakish charm of Mr. Butler, the carpetbagging, damsel-baiting, swoon-worthy leading man of *Gone With the Wind*. The problem is, everyone associates the name with the character, which may settle a bit awkwardly on, say, a chubby accountant. It's one of those names that's almost too romantic. (Think Romeo.) It puts a lot of undue pressure on a young man making his way in the world. It's also ever-so-slightly feminine.

Riley: A bouncy, grinning Irish surname, Riley is a hit for both boys and girls. Although the girls currently have the lead, it's been fairly common as a masculine first name for at least a hundred years or more. That said, think long and hard before you dub your son something that could be on the top 20 girls list soon. On the upside, people love this name for its friendly, congenial nature. Riley Henderson was a boy who briefly takes up residence in a tree house in Truman Capote's novel *The Grass Harp*.

Roark: Calling all architecture buffs or fans of Ayn Rand's novel *The Fountainhead*—we've got something just for you. Howard Roark, played by Gary Cooper in the movie version, is an idealistic young architect. Short of a Howard revival, this fascinating character's last name is the grounded-yet-offbeat moniker to choose.

Robinson: Similar to Morrison and Morris, Robinson has a ring that is infinitely zestier than Rob or—heavens no!—Robin. It has the surname style of Sullivan or MacKenzie yet brings an extra dash of adventure vis à vis *Robinson Crusoe*, Daniel Defoe's tale of a shipwrecked castaway who faces mutineers, savages, and wild animals before being rescued. Baseball legend Jackie Robinson adds a Hall of Fame edge, too.

Roman: Okay, so this isn't a character name per se, but Roman was the name for countless extras in Shakespearean productions. It means simply "citizen of Rome," and with several of his plays set in Italy, the Bard had plenty of use for Romans. As a first name, Roman is unusually strong, robust, and full of vitality. It's old school and newfangled at the same time. This winner was picked by both Cate Blanchett and Debra Messing.

Romeo: On what planet do parents pick this insanely starry-eyed name? The universe of soccer star David Beckham and his wife, Posh Spice, which is to say, not really on the same green earth as the rest of us. Posh and Becks can probably pull it off with their middle son, but mere mortals should approach this red-hot name with caution. You might hope your child is well liked by the girls when he's, say, ready to ask someone to the prom, but with a name this intense, the pressure is on to be far more slick and fabulous then any teenage boy should be. Shakespeare tried to invent names that conjured up certain feelings or images, so it shouldn't be a surprise that Romeo is taken from the word for romance.

Roth: You'll be sure to raise eyebrows with this iconoclastic choice, but your peerless progeny will also have a one-of-a-kind name. (If the old school gets disconcerted, you might want to mention "Seth" as a comforting reference.) In an age of Riley, Keegan, and Hunter, why not adopt this Jewish surname? Philip Roth is one of the most lauded American writers of his time. A recipient of the National Book Award and the Pulitzer Prize, he is the author of such works as *The Human Stain*.

Rupert: On the one hand, Rupert is stately, conservative, and classical, but there's a cuddly side to this, too. In England, there are oodles of Ruperts. Young Englishman Rupert Grint (Ron from the Harry Potter films) has brought an impish, red-haired look to the name, while suave Rupert Everett imparts sophistication. Stateside, Rupert was Veruca Salt's father in *Charlie and the Chocolate Factory*, and the name of the guy who sang "The Piña Colada Song" (just a random fun fact for you). This name goes beautifully with some of the other cute-yet-urbane names on the rise, such as Leo, Milo, and August.

Ryder: Once upon a time, a beautiful movie star and her beautifully grungy (i.e., hip-yet-odd-looking) music star husband had a bouncing rock baby boy and named him Ryder. The baby grew into a much-photographed, much-discussed, long-haired beautiful rock boy, and his previously obscure name hurtled from nowhere everywhere. It became a superhip name studded with rock 'n' roll energy and sprinkled with movie star fairy dust. The end. Oh, and a couple of centuries before Ryder Robinson, offspring of Kate Hudson and Chris Robinson, was born, there was a book called *Brideshead Revisited: The Sacred & Profane Memories of Captain Charles Ryder*.

Salinger: Devoted readers (and there is a legion of them) of J. D. Salinger's *The Catcher in the Rye* might deliberate his surname as an overtly literary tribute name. But, it does have a hip, swinging sound that fits nicely with other popular surnames such as Sawyer and Sullivan. Why not pay tribute to the iconic (and reclusive) author who found his way into every teenage boy's soul through his depiction of alienated prep-school castoff Holden Caulfield? Sal is a nifty short form, too.

Nickname: Sal

Samuel: At this point I know four Samuel and Benjamin brother combos, and I am sure there are many more all over North America. In my unscientific survey, most people start with Sam, having no idea how common it is. By the time Ben comes around, they know that both names are as ordinary as soccer balls on the playground, and they don't care. Why? Sam still sounds cool and creative. He can be a smarty, a jock, a quiet kid, or a jokester. Unaccountably, Sam can do it all with one hand tied behind his handsome little back. In terms of legacy, Samuel is biblical, presidential, and all over the great books, such as Samuel Taylor Coleridge ("The Rime of the Ancient Mariner"). **Sam** Spade, of course, was Dashiell Hammett's original hard-boiled detective. Perhaps Charlie Sheen and Tiger Woods liked the crisp brevity of Spade's first name: they both named their daughters Sam.

Saul: Saul is an old-time Jewish name that's open to all for consideration, along with names like Eli, Reuben, and Isaiah. Short and punchy, Saul would make quite a fashion statement, although it's never completely faded out of style or use. In the Bible, Saul was the first king of Israel and David's father-in-law. Saul was also the original name of the apostle Paul. Saul Bellow was the Chicago novelist whose works, including *The Adventures of Augie March*, won him the Nobel Prize for literature in 1976.

Sawyer: One of my favorite surname names, amiable Sawyer is both modern and old-fashioned, boasts a rugged, rustic charm, and is remarkably untrendy. In fact, its style meshes well with top 100 favorites Wyatt and Hayden, but it's far less used. Sawyer takes a page from Twain's children's chestnut, which details the boyhood capers of Tom Sawyer and his friend Huckleberry Finn. Though the name Huckleberry has a more overt tie to the book, Sawyer does conjure up a fun smidgen of mischief. This is a wonderful, warm name with charm and friendliness to spare.

Wyatt and Hayden are cool, but Sawyer conjures up an extra fun smidgen of mischief à la Tom and Huck.

Sayers: Here's an undiscovered option that could be quite the find if you're seeking originality and a literary link. Sayer (minus the last *s*) is a tradesman name that means "professional storyteller," and it's a heartbeat away from the trendy Sawyer. Add an *s* to the end and you could be paying tribute to Dorothy Sayers, the British mystery writer best known for her sleuthing stories featuring English aristocrat Lord Peter Wimsey. She was also an adjunct member of the Inklings, the famed writers group formed by C. S. Lewis at Oxford.

Scott: Like Jay, Doug, and Chad, Scott seems locked into the 1960s. Guys who have these kinds of names are usually *coaching* the soccer team, not kicking the ball. But for parents who have a taste for the reliable and unswerving—not those who are keen on reviving some Victorian antique such as Phineas or Oliver—Scott is a nice, middle-of-the-road option. F. (Francis) Scott Key Fitzgerald went through life as Scott to all who knew him. He is regarded as one of the greatest twentieth-century writers and the king of the Jazz Age, a term he himself coined.

Seamus: Where do you go when you've met too many little guys named Riley, Connor, or even Liam? To Declan, Cormac, and Seamus, of course. These convivial Irish names pack a serious Emerald Isle punch. Seamus ("SHAY-mus"), like Sean, has the "sha" sound, which will confuse people only for a little while. (They're used to Sean, after all.) Hopefully you have a vibrantly

> Convivial Irish names like Seamus pack a serious Emerald Isle punch.

Irish surname, because Seamus Wolenski might give folks whiplash. Seamus Justin Heaney is the Irish poet, writer, and lecturer from County Londonderry, Northern Ireland. He was awarded the Nobel Prize in literature in 1995 and is considered the best Irish poet since Yeats.

Sebastian: Here we have a top 100 name that somehow sounds like an obscure, quirky find. Someone with this European-sounding handle will be expected to be handsome, smart, and most likely artistic. He'll be that cute guy who says the slyest things in your English lit class, who then ends up restoring rare books for a living. Sebastian was Viola's twin brother in *Twelfth Night*. Frequently mistaken for Cesario (his sister disguised as a guy), the dude ends up marrying the beautiful Lady Olivia. If you love it, take heart: Sebastian isn't for everyone. It's too rarefied and Renaissance to go all Wal-Mart on us. I predict it will never crack the top 50.

Silas: Miraculously, Silas has not cracked the top 400—yet. It's flat-out gorgeous, not to mention funky and dashing with a pinch of homespun charm. Silas was the protagonist of George Eliot's humdinger of a novel *Silas Marner*. The biblical Silas was a missionary with quite a humdinger of a story himself. (See Acts 15:26, 27.) Seriously, folks, don't leave this stunning bargain on the shelf if you are seeking a novel name for your singular son. It's a country-fried, old-coot name that will sound like a total hepcat on a little boy nibbling on sushi in Manhattan.

Spenser: This noble name has a little extra elegance over its surname brethren, such as Jackson and Hunter. Its veneer makes it especially sophisticated. If you're looking for a rugged, rustic name, this is not it. And like Cooper or Peyton, Spenser sounds just the slightest bit preppy. If that bothers you, think about Sawyer or Sullivan, which both seem more grounded. Those might be fresher options, as Spenser (in the Spencer spelling) spiked in popularity in the nineties. Edmund Spenser, of course, wrote the fantastical epic poem *The Faerie Queene*.

Starbuck: Line up, iconoclasts (and coffee lovers), for the ultimate barista name. Starbuck was the young, Quaker first mate of the *Moby-Dick* ship, *The Pequod*. (Did you know that Herman Melville based his title character mammal on a real-life sperm whale named Mocha Dick? Starbuck...Mocha...coincidence? I don't think so.) Starbuck is also linked to sci-fi as a *Battlestar Galactica* favorite.

Sully: A spry and jolly name, Sully sounds like a guy who makes friends easily and is full of self-confidence and joie de vivre. Kids will instantly make the connection between a human Sully and the loveable *Monsters Inc.* furry guy, which is a nifty link your Sully will appreciate when he's a cartoon-watching tyke. You can always lengthen it to **Sullivan**, like

---

Pre-Vogue

(i.e.: What're you waiting for?
Get while the getting's good!)

Asher ✷ August ✷ Beckett ✷ Curran ✷ Ezra
✷ Jasper ✷ Langston ✷ Lincoln ✷ Miller ✷ Truman

Patrick Dempsey ("McDreamy") did with one of his twin boys. René-François-Armand (Sully) Prudhomme was a French poet and essayist, and the winner of the first Nobel Prize in literature in 1901.

🐰 T 🐰

Tarquin: Here we have a fantastic discovery that is, unfortunately, linked to a big literary baddie (more on him later). Tarquin is a gorgeous name with striking Roman good looks. It's like Julius or Marcus but much more surprising and novel. Two kings of ancient Rome, including Tarquin the Proud, have worn this moniker, making it a nice historical find. With that hot *quin* ending (a perfect nickname, by the way), Tarquin is in a class all by itself. But back to the baddie: Tarquin was the villain of Shakespeare's poem "The Rape of Lucrece." The good news? Who reads that thing anyway?
   Nicknames: Tarq, Quin

Tennyson: I concur with actor Russell Crowe and his wife, Danielle Spencer, that Tennyson is a grand thing to call a boy (or possibly even a girl, see Tennyson, page 92). Not only does it dovetail nicely with the surname craze (think Sullivan, Grayson, or Paxton), but it takes a stuffy butler's handle, flips it, and makes it neat-o on a little boy. Tennyson means "son of Dennis," a nice little bonus if, in fact, the father's name is Dennis. In any case, it's a poetic, rich name with a built-in nickname (Tenny).
   Nicknames: Ten, Tenny

Thatcher: A cross between Theodore and Fletcher, Thatcher is a cool-sounding surname with loads of potential. Once an occupational ID for someone who thatched roofs for a living, Thatcher has that cozy, once-upon-a-time vibe people are so crazy about these days. With Hunter, Tyler, and Carter climbing the charts, you can sneak in on the trend with this rarely used and more interesting choice. Bonus: Thatcher will be familiar to readers of *The Adventures of Tom Sawyer* as the last name of Tom's gal pal, Becky, and her dad, Judge Thatcher.

Theodore: If most of the old standbys don't ring your bell, but you have a more conservative taste, take a look at Theodore. It boasts a verve and creativity that most stalwarts like Peter, Andrew, and John can't touch. The chief asset of this name is its fabulous short form: Theo brims with warmth, energy, and that yummy *o* ending. Though a viable nickname, I'd stay away from Ted—doesn't he sound like a life insurance salesman with too much hair product? Theodore Dreiser wrote *Sister Carrie*, among other novels, and there's also Fyodor (the Russian shape of Theodore) Dostoyevsky, the literary great who penned *Crime and Punishment* and *The Brothers Karamazov*.

Nicknames: Theo, Teddy

Thomas: Ah, good old Thomas. This old reliable has never gone out of fashion, and for that matter, it's never dipped below 50 on the popularity chart. (There's a reason people use "every Tom, Dick, and Harry" as a colloquialism invoking the everyday guy.) It's a handsome classic with integrity, a name taken seriously because of its biblical and presidential roots but with a boy-next-door vibe. One way to jazz up Thomas is to pick a quirkier middle name, like Creed or Herman or Obadiah. There are lots of Thomases in literature, including Dylan Thomas, Thomas Aquinas, Thomas a Kempis, and Thomas the Tank Engine.

Thor: This may be the "Don't mess with me" name of all time. It boldly declares that your people came from Scandanavia, probably on a Viking ship, and they were really hairy and scary and did a lot of raiding and pillaging in their horned helmets. Still, there have been Thors spotted in recent years sucking their thumbs and carrying sippy cups. Thor is the red-haired, bearded god of thunder in Norse mythology. If red hair runs in your family, even better.

Thornton: Thornton is built like an old coot—think Thaddeus, Truman, Chester, Phinneaus—but it's coated with a more literary sheen. It's a big, fusty name that seems to be wearing spectacles and smoking a pipe. In the right hands, Thornton could be turned on its stodgy ear to sound positively hip. The lit gloss, of course, comes from the brilliant American author and playwright Thornton Wilder, whose best known works include *The Bridge of San Luis Rey*, his 1927 novel, and *Our Town*, the 1938 play. Both won Wilder the Pulitzer Prize.
   Nickname: Thorn

Timon: There are usable cartoon names (Ariel, Sully, and Dash are three), but I'm not sure you'd want your child affiliated so thoroughly with the jittery meercat of *The Lion King* fame. (I can just hear the peanut gallery now: "If you have another boy will you name him Pumbaa?") Can you handle that reference? Yes? Well, you can always tell people he's named after Timon of Athens, immortalized in a play by Shakespeare.

Titus: Old Roman and Greek relics are definitely warming: Marcus is a player, Tristan's a hot hit, and now Julius and Matthias are flickering. Titus is caught in the updraft and is slowly ascending. Titus was one of Saint Paul's "pastoral epistles," which makes this a singular biblical choice as well. In literature, *Titus Andronicus* is thought to be Shakespeare's earliest tragedy, and it's most definitely his bloodiest. It leaves out no gory detail of the battle between Titus and Queen Tamora the Goth.

Tristan: If you go weak in the knees at the mere mention of Tristan and Isolde, you're not alone. Since the twelfth century, the legend of the Cornish knight Tristan and his love, the Irish princess Isolde, has been told and retold in numerous poems and stories. Some scholars think Tristan and Isolde's love story inspired the tale of Lancelot and Guinevere. Are we not all swooning collectively? That's part of the issue with the name, which may be too mushy for your manly man. Try renting *Legends of the Fall*, the Brad Pitt movie based on the Jim Harrison novel that all guys pretty much dig. Brad-as-Tristan brings a certain rugged, wilderness quality to the whole thing, if you can believe it. James Franco as Tristan in 2006's *Tristan and Isolde* ain't too shabby either.

Troy: We all know at least one Troy who is pushing forty or fifty, so this blond, muscular name may need a few more decades before coming back into fashion. However, Brad Pitt helped reinvent the name by appearing in *Troy*, a movie about the Trojan War. (He's so helpful in these matters. See Tristan.) Troy is a place-name in literature: it's the location of one of the most important events in Greek mythology, the Trojan War, which was written about by Homer in *The Iliad* and *The Odyssey*. Today it is an archeological heritage site in modern-day Turkey.

Truman: Truman seems poised for a comeback, even though it was never really a hit. It peaked in the 300s circa 1924, when Truman Capote was born. It definitely has some components to launch it to a higher orbit of popularity: it's presidential, an old coot, and a celebrity pick (Tom Hanks and Rita Wilson, ace baby namers, have a Truman), plus, with the influx of Capote-related films in recent years, we've been hearing it often. The nickname True packs everything you could ever want for your child into one resonant syllable. How can it miss? Truman Capote is recognized as a literary icon, having written such classics as *Breakfast at Tiffany's* and *In Cold Blood*.

> The nickname True packs everything you could ever want for your child into one resonant syllable.

Twain: It rhymes with a bunch of familiar names—Wayne, Duane, or Shane—but it's miles more exciting. Whether or not you listen to country music, Shania's surname adds a cool cowboy kick. Essentially, though, this would be a big tip of the hat to Mark Twain, the American literary giant who still looms large through such iconic works as *The Adventures of Huckleberry Finn*. Along with Huckleberry and Sawyer, Twain is a freckle-faced, barefoot kind of name that sounds just right to propel a modern boy on a lifetime of adventure.

Ulysses: If you don't give a fig what the neighbors, your family, or anyone else thinks, allocate Ulysses for your no doubt intrepid child. The roots of this name—the Latin form of Odysseus—date back many millennia, and thus the name itself carries a historical gravity intensified by the Civil War general and American president Ulysses S. Grant. In literature, Ulysses is well worn as the title of both James Joyce's epic novel and Alfred, Lord Tennyson's poem about the heroic king of Ithica. Lys won't work as a nickname, but what about just U? Maybe even Uly. Maybe. If this is your choice, look at it this way: the relatives won't bat an eye when Homer and Calliope join the clan.

Nicknames: U, Uly

Victor: One cool factoid right off the bat: Victor is one of two names I know that became more popular because a famous female, in this case Queen Victoria, inspired people to name their babies after her. (Mario, a variation of Mary, is the other one.) Can't you just see people's expressions when you tell them your linebacker was named after a queen? Okay, so this probably won't be the reason you dub your son Victor, but it's still a nifty tidbit. Moving along... Victor is a distinguished, old-fashioned appellation that has an almost Pan-European feel, as almost every country has Victors in it. Since there is a Nick on every soccer team these days, it's not such a leap to Vic, and it's certainly more novel. Victor Hugo wrote *Les Misérables*.

Nickname: Vic

Vidal: The intriguing name would hold more appeal if it didn't instantly make one think of shampoo and conditioner. Who knows? Maybe on the right tyke Vidal could take on a life beyond hair guru Sassoon. At least it's better than the novelist, screenwriter, and playwright Vidal's first name, Gore, as in "gory details" or "guts and gore."

Virgil: Virgil is a fantastically fusty name, which means it should hold great appeal for fans of Oscar, Gus, Silas, and all the other gruff grandpa names that are so hot these days. It also boasts a supreme literary lineage, going back to the first century BC when Virgil wrote *The Aeneid*, the poem that became the Roman Empire's national epic. But then there's the little matter of *Virg*, a prefix which causes the name to verge on cruel in our hyperhormonal society. Publius Vergilius, Virgil's full name, does not help.

Out on a Long Limb

Ajax ❖ Booker ❖ Gulliver ❖ Homer ❖ Ibsen
❖ Jupiter ❖ Linus ❖ Nemo ❖ Ovid ❖ Ulysses

 W

Walden: Presenting the ultimate environmental name, from the book of the same name about Henry David Thoreau's two years, two months, and two days in the forest around Walden Pond. Of course, Walden was more than a woodsy memoir; it was a social critique that rings true to this day. Famously, Thoreau said, "If a man does not keep pace with his companions, perhaps it is because he hears the beat of a different drummer." Parents who hear that beat can consider this a like-minded find.

> Presenting Walden, the ultimate environmental name, from the book of the same name about Henry David Thoreau's two years, two months, and two days in the forest around Walden Pond.

Walker: Walker is cut from the same tradesman cloth as Fletcher or Cooper and could conceivably rise as a cool entry in the surname category. Should you be wondering what a walker did, the name comes from the medieval profession of a person who stomped on woolen cloth in a bath of clay to thicken the fibers and ready the cloth for use. (Who knew?) Walker Percy was the Southern author of such works as *The Moviegoer*, which won the National Book Award for fiction in 1962.

Walter: An audacious baby namer I know can't wait to reawaken Walter from a one-hundred-year slumber (a century ago, this noble name was in the top 15), but she keeps having girls. To some—okay, most—Walter sounds like a man wearing a cardigan, puttering in his garden. To others, like Julia Roberts, who gave her son Phinneaus the middle name Walter, this is starting to have a retro-cool ring to it. To use this classic, take a page from Walter Mitty's book and imagine the possibilities, one of which is the cozy nickname Walt, as in Whitman.

Nicknames: Walt, Wally

Walton: If you don't want to go quite as far as Walter but like the general sound, Walton could make a peaceable, relaxed, and homespun choice. After all, it's a surname people associate with all things related to hearth and home, with the cozy image of John Boy Walton saying goodnight to Jim Bob, Mary Ellen, and all the folks at bedtime. The literary Walton adds an image of fishing, too. Izaak Walton's 1653 treatise on worms and hooks and flies and rivers, *The Compleat Angler*, is still beloved today.

Nickname: Walt

Washington: Washington would definitely take more daring than Lincoln, Truman, or even Wilson, the presidential names that have heated up in the last few years. Some baby-name experts are passing on this heavy appellation, but I think it could work in the right family. It's vibrantly patriotic and much more connected to founding father George Washington than his first name. It's a big, old, historically imposing name, but if you're still game, my hat's off to you. Washington Irving was an American author of the early nineteenth century. Best known for his short stories "The

Legend of Sleepy Hollow" and "Rip Van Winkle" (both of which appear in his book *The Sketch Book of Geoffrey Crayon*), he was also a mentor to Nathaniel Hawthorne, Henry Wadsworth Longfellow, and Edgar Allan Poe.

Whitman: Like Dexter, Truman, and Chester, it's hip to be square with an old coot such as Whitman. This could work for parents who want to resuscitate a creaky moniker and give it a brand-new life on a cute little kid. Picture a five-year-old Whitman: what do you see? I see round glasses, a bug collection, and a terrific sense of humor. Whit is a snappy little nickname, too. In "Leaves of Grass," Walt Whitman wrote, "Rhymes and rhymers pass away...America justifies itself, give it time." Give Whitman time to justify itself, and it surely will.

Nickname: Whit

William: A William by any other name—would he still have become the Bard? We'll never know, but we can thank Mr. Shakespeare for creating so many fabulous names for his plays, and for giving us a rock-solid, lit-hero name for the ages. William is one of my favorite classics, a stalwart yet comfy name that still holds tons of appeal and boasts so much versatility. In this day and age, few people are going to reduce William to Bill or **Billy** (although Billy Coleman was the charming key character of *Where the Red Fern Grows*). Modern parents are going with Will or William. (Willy? Maybe, if you can't help yourself when faced with a precious bouncing baby boy.) Princess Diana called her prince Wills, and doesn't he, the future king of England, enhance his regal appellation even more? To inject some global verve in the basic William model, try an ethnic spin, such as the engaging Willem (Dutch/German) or the hot Liam (Irish).

   Nicknames: Will, Willy, Bill, Billy

Wilson: Like Jackson and Carter, Wilson just might have a shot at the big time as one of the most viable and handsome presidential names. *Where the Red Fern Grows* author Wilson Rawls (born Woodrow Wilson Rawls) was born six months after President Wilson took office—apparently the author's mother and father were big fans. Almost one hundred years later, the name Wilson still holds plenty of appeal. You can honor a beloved William in a roundabout way, as both names yield the great nickname Will. Wilson has more homespun, barefoot allure than William's stateliness.

   Nickname: Will

Wolfe: *Look Homeward Angel* was great and all, but Thomas Wolfe's surname may be too fanged and furry to consider. Journalist Wolf Blitzer has set a precedent, though, if you really dig it.

Wyatt: Here's a smashing name, brimming with the cowboy ruggedness and hottie looks of a Western movie hero. When you turn that Wyatt Earp/cowpoke thing inside out and hang his ten-gallon on a city boy, the charm is undeniable. The only caveat with this name is that it's rising none too slowly up the list and could easily be a top 20 blockbuster someday. Thomas Wyatt wasn't a cowboy, but he was a poet, one of England's first to use the sonnet form for his poetry. His poem "Whoso list to hunt" is believed to be about Anne Boleyn, whom Wyatt loved and lost to Henry VIII.

Nickname: Wy

Yeats: An Irish poet, whose works gave expression to the spirit of his homeland? Sounds wildly romantic, artistic, and exhilarating, and maybe a touch belligerent. William Butler Yeats, of course, was the Nobel Prize–winning poet of such works as "The Second Coming" and "Lake Isle of Innisfree." The poet from County Sligo was mystical, political, and one of a kind. Naming your child Yeats would definitely be an almost singular action, although I've heard it as a middle name. If you're looking for something short, punchy, and meaningful to fill that middle slot with more than mere filler, Yeats is a stunner.

> If you're looking for something short, punchy, and meaningful to fill that middle slot with more then mere filler, Yeats is a stunner.

Zachary: Zachary was embraced wholeheartedly by parents in the nineties, and it's still a top 50 name. But, like other nineties sensations Spencer, Tyler, and Ryan, Zachary is losing some zip. There's nothing cooler than a Z

If you like Zach, consider Zane, Zander, Zebedee, and Zeke.

name, though, so do consider zestier options such as Zane, Zander, Zebedee, and Zeke. Zachary was a member of J. D. Salinger's Glass family, about whom he wrote many short stories and the novella *Franny and Zooey*. Zooey was actually Zachary Glass's nickname.

Zane: Happy trails are ahead for parents looking to rope a name fit for a rugged cowboy. Zane shares a lot of Wild West qualities with Zach but is about ten times less popular, a bonus for admirers of the letter Z who want something more bold. Zane Grey (given name: Pearl—ouch) was a big game fisherman, a minor league baseball player, and the wildly popular author of such pulp fiction Westerns as *Riders of the Purple Sage*. He also is credited by some as coming up with the original idea for the Lone Ranger.

Index

About the Author

LORILEE CRAKER is the author of ten books, including *Date Night in a Minivan: Revving Up Your Marriage After the Kids Arrive* and *Pop Culture Mom: A Real Story of Fame and Family in a Tabloid Age*, with Lynne Spears. She speaks at moms groups and retreats regularly from her home in West Michigan, where she also moonlights as an entertainment reporter for the *Grand Rapids Press*. Lorilee is married to Doyle and they have three children, Jonah, Ezra, and Phoebe.